THE BURIED CITY

Gabriel Zuchtriegel is Director General of the archaeological park in Pompeii. He studied classical archaeology at the Humboldt University in Berlin and received his PhD from the University of Bonn. In 2015, he became director of the Paestum archaeological park and museum, before being appointed at Pompeii in February 2021. He became an Italian citizen in 2020 and is currently overseeing the biggest dig of the site of Pompeii in a generation.

THE BURIED CITY

Unearthing the Real Pompeii

GABRIEL ZUCHTRIEGEL

translated from the German by Jamie Bulloch

hodder
press

First published in 2023 by Propyläen Verlag
First published in Great Britain in 2025 by Hodder Press
An imprint of Hodder & Stoughton Limited
An Hachette UK company

Copyright © Ullstein Buchverlage GmbH, Berlin, 2025.

Translation Copyright © Jamie Bulloch 2025.

The right of Gabriel Zuchtriegel to be identified as the Author of the Work has been asserted by him in accordance with the Copyright, Designs and Patents Act 1988.

Images:
Plate sections: © p. 1: National Archaeological Museum of Napoli, Ministry of Culture; all others: Archaeological Park of Pompeii, Ministry of Culture. Photos: Silvia Vacca (p. 2, 3, 4 (below), 5, 6–15, 17–23, 29, 30); Llorenç Alapont (p. 28, below); Giuseppe Sannino (p. 1); Luigi Spina (p. 24, above-left and below); Archaeological Park of Pompeii Press Office (p. 16, 24 (above-right), 25 (below), 28 (above), 31, 32); Gabriel Zuchtriegel (p. 4 (above), 25 (above), 26, 27). Maps: Simona Capecchi (p. viii of text); Raffaele Martinelli (p. 18 of plate sections, below).

All rights reserved. No part of this publication may be reproduced, stored in a retrieval system, or transmitted, in any form or by any means without the prior written permission of the publisher, nor be otherwise circulated in any form of binding or cover other than that in which it is published and without a similar condition being imposed on the subsequent purchaser.

A CIP catalogue record for this title is available from the British Library.

Hardback ISBN 9781399731171
Trade Paperback ISBN 9781399741729
ebook ISBN 9781399731188

Typeset in Minion Pro by Hewer Text UK Ltd, Edinburgh
Printed and bound in Great Britain by Clays Ltd, Elcograf S.p.A.

Hodder & Stoughton policy is to use papers that are natural, renewable and recyclable products and made from wood grown in sustainable forests. The logging and manufacturing processes are expected to conform to the environmental regulations of the country of origin.

Hodder & Stoughton Limited
Carmelite House
50 Victoria Embankment
London EC4Y 0DZ

The authorised representative in the EEA is Hachette Ireland, 8 Castlecourt Centre, Dublin 15, D15 XTP3, Ireland (email: info@hbgi.ie)

www.hodderpress.co.uk

Pompeii like any other town. Same old humanity. All the same whether one be dead or alive. Pompeii comfortable sermon. Like Pompeii better than Paris.

         Herman Melville, *Journal*, 1857

CONTENTS

Map of Pompeii — viii

Introduction: Risks and side-effects — 1
1 What is it about classical art? — 17
2 Captivating rituals — 65
3 A city on the verge of catastrophe — 121
4 What counts in the end — 173
5 Life goes on — 211
Afterword — 219

Acknowledgements — 229
Notes — 233
Index — 237

House of the Vettii

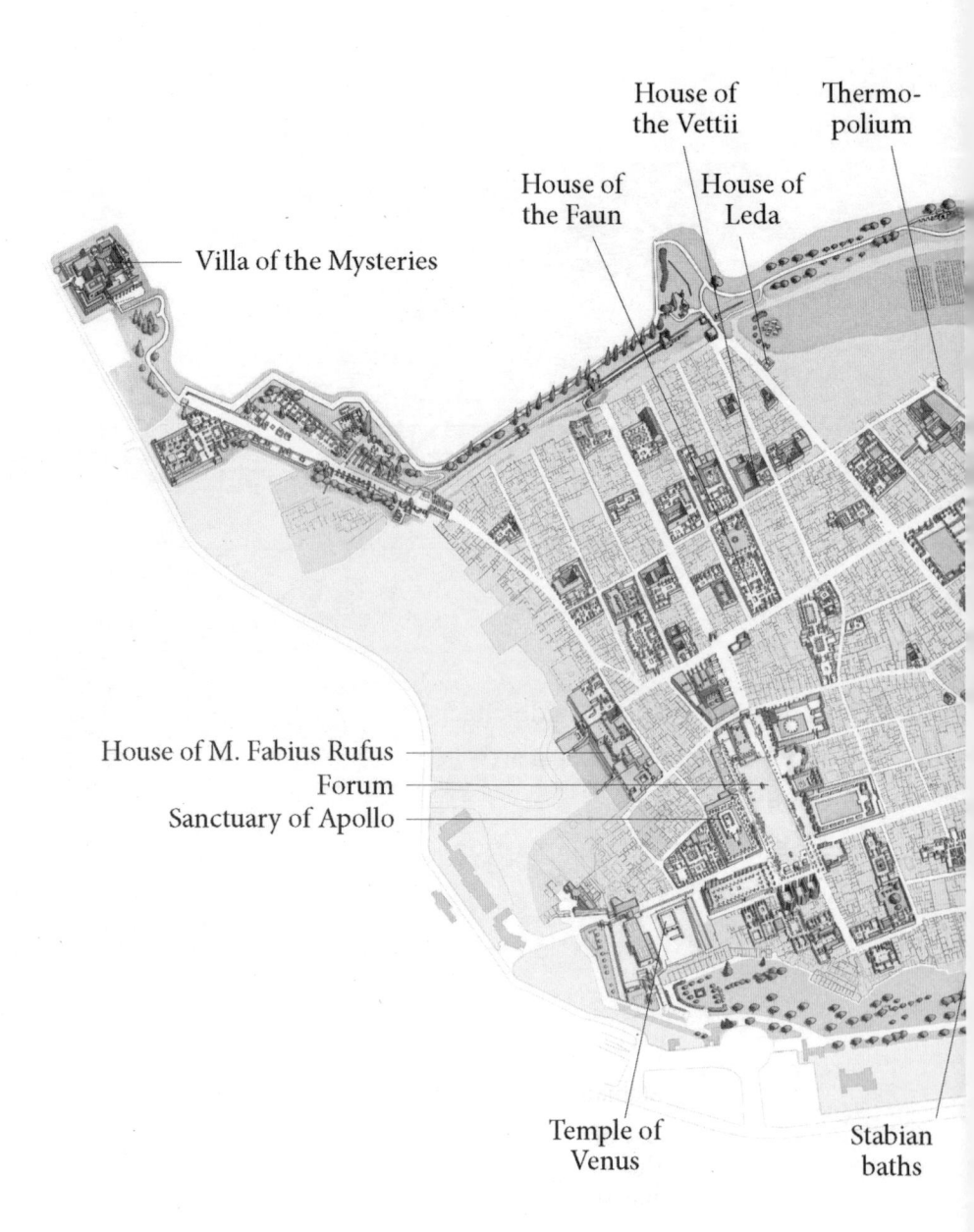

Thermopolium

House of the Faun

House of Leda

Villa of the Mysteries

House of M. Fabius Rufus
Forum
Sanctuary of Apollo

Temple of Venus

Stabian baths

House of the
Lararium

Sarno Gate

Amphi-
theatre

Garden of the
Fugitives

House of
Menander

Stabian Gate

Temple   Theatre   House of
of Athena   the
                    Citharist

INTRODUCTION
RISKS AND SIDE-EFFECTS

I didn't know that visitors to Pompeii regularly suffer heart attacks, some with fatal consequences, until I was quietly told so by an experienced employee. This was a few weeks after I'd taken up my role as director of the UNESCO World Heritage Site and since then we've ramped up the emergency medical provision in the ancient city. An average of 600 people require treatment each year, twenty per cent of whom suffer heart and circulation problems. These cases are usually put down to the hot weather. But is that the only reason?

In 2018 one visitor to the Uffizi Gallery in Florence suffered a heart attack in front of Botticelli's *The Birth of Venus* in a fully air-conditioned room. The media speculated that this might be a case of Stendhal syndrome, named after the French writer who in 1817 visited the Basilica di Santa Croce in Florence and experienced a sort of ecstasy when confronted by all the church's art and history. In the 1970s the Florentine psychiatrist Graziella Magherini detected similar symptoms in tourists to the city. 'Stendhal syndrome' was born.[1] As it's not recognised as an official medical condition, the list of symptoms is open-ended.

THE BURIED CITY

Apart from heart attacks, these include: palpitations, breathing difficulties and hyperventilation, fainting, giddiness, sweating, nausea and hallucinations.

So far, I have been spared. But there are some places in Pompeii where I spy potential dangers. These include the *Orto dei Fuggiaschi*, the 'Garden of the Fugitives', on the southern fringes of the ancient city. Here archaeologists discovered thirteen victims of the volcanic eruption that, on an autumn day in 79 CE, buried Pompeii beneath a metre-thick layer of ashes. Around 7.30 in the morning, almost twenty hours after the beginning of the eruption, they died trying to escape the city. Struck by a wave of heat of around 200 degrees Celsius, surging from the nearby volcano of Vesuvius at almost 100 kilometres per hour, they were knocked to the floor. Several of them are holding up their hands to protect their faces, while one man is summoning the last of his strength trying to get to his feet. A small boy is clutching his chest, impotent against the force of the shockwave of dust and ash that enveloped him. He almost seems to be sleeping, his mouth slightly open.

These are thirteen of the 1,300 victims of the eruption excavated to date in Pompeii. But thirteen whose facial features, clothes, physiques we know precisely, as if they'd been dead just a few hours. Ash and dust hardened around their bodies, which decomposed, leaving a cavity in the ground.

When excavators came across these cavities between April and June 1961, they filled them with plaster. And so, after nineteen centuries, the casts of these people are before us once more. Or rather than casts, are they actually the individuals themselves? How should we deal with such 'finds'? And what does the way we deal with them say about ourselves?

In Pompeii questions like these sometimes arise specifically. For example, when I'm showing a group of potential sponsors from the Naples Chamber of Commerce and Industry (CCI) around Pompeii, which I did a few weeks after my arrival. Here they are again, those expectant faces, who seem to be saying, 'Come on, tell us why we're actually here. Prove to us it was worth the journey.' Should I include the children, women and men from the 'Garden of the Fugitives' in my tour, try to share my emotions with the people from the CCI? Or would that be a kind of betrayal? If I spoke about the thirteen victims, would I be divulging something intimate about myself too? If one of the visitors were struck down by Stendhal syndrome, wouldn't that make me partially responsible?

This book answers 'Yes!' to all of these questions. For in my career as an archaeologist, from tourist guide at Berlin's Pergamon Museum during my student days all the way to Pompeii, I've realised that Stendhal syndrome isn't the problem. Statistically, heart attacks and other medical emergencies don't occur more frequently in Pompeii than in your average pedestrian zone. The problem is a different one; let's call it collector syndrome.

The collector views everything from the perspective of possession. Would that be a good addition to my collection? Does someone else have more than me? A constant weighing up, accumulating, comparing, assessing, judging. They see the world as a sort of warehouse where the aim is to fill their trolley to the brim, so far as their credit card allows.

Time and again I've met people who own collections of antiquities and, believe me, I haven't envied a single one of them. On the contrary I've pitied them for reducing such a wonderful thing as archaeology to a pile of possessions. But collector syndrome isn't restricted to collectors of antiquities. We all suffer from it to a certain degree; it's simply a manifestation of our materialistic world.

A study has shown that two of the most important motivations for visiting a museum are the accumulation of knowledge and of experience.[2] If you read more closely, it turns out that 'accumulating experience' means ticking things off: visit Pompeii – done! The experiences that need to be ticked off are selected on the basis of what people hear or read. In other words, this group is going where you have to have visited. You work your way through a list. What? Never been to the Louvre? Get down there quick, otherwise you're not a whole person/archaeologist/art historian. Collector syndrome means you live in the awareness that there's still somewhere you have to go, something else you have to become, something else you need to get your hands on, whether it be knowledge, experience or possession.

I would go so far as to say that this collecting is the strongest motive – judging, at least, by the majority of visitors I've met as a guide in archaeological museums and parks. First and foremost they want to know why that place is on their list.

RISKS AND SIDE-EFFECTS

The need to tick things off is, of course, brilliantly sustained by social media. My grandparents would have thought it highly amusing that people film things before they even look at them. But these days we're so used to it. It's also perfectly fine; I mean, we don't want to start telling people what to do.

But it's quite different when it comes to another symptom of collector syndrome: people taking things away with them. Every week packets and parcels arrive at Pompeii containing pumice, mosaic tesserae or sherds that someone has pinched. The remorse comes years, sometimes decades later – the downside of collecting is that what people accumulate eventually proves to be a burden. In Pompeii, moreover, there's a legend going around that walking off with such objects – which, by the way, is a prosecutable offence – brings bad luck. Many a rueful collector accompanies their returned goods with a list of misfortunes, some of which are quite touching. I've read about divorces, job dismissals and even cancer diagnoses. Here's an example from summer 2022:

> Dear museum manager,
>
> I am a rock collector and everywhere I go I pick up a rock or a small stone. So when I went to Pompeii in 2012 I picked up these and a little piece of ceramic I found on the floor.
>
> A while ago I read an article in CNN and also in The Lonely Planet where they talk about people returning the stones they took because they brought them bad luck. Since then I've been haunted by these stories.
>
> I began going back in time and I definitely feel that since 2012 things in my life & career haven't been working well. I am even going through complicated health issues up to now.

THE BURIED CITY

> I don't know if the 'curse' is true or not, but I decided to send back these objects to where they belong.

To which group would Stendhal have belonged? Definitely not a group of collectors; during his life he was a restless wayfarer with little space for clutter, be it material or intellectual. We can also rule out another group, which according to the study is relatively large – those who go to museums to please their partners – to say nothing of those whose principal reason for the visit is to use the lavatory. (They do indeed constitute a group, albeit a reassuringly small one.)

Stendhal would have fitted best in the group that experts describe as 'spiritual pilgrims'.[3] They visit a museum or archaeological park to refuel, to get to know themselves better, find inspiration and a sense of freedom. To discover something new, like a child, for the first time. Not working through the highlights as defined by others, but trusting their own perception. In this way a museum visit can indeed become a spiritual experience. Because the point is to transcend yourself. Stendhal spoke of 'heavenly feelings' that accompany a total 'exhaustion' of the self.[4] That might sound a bit pompous today, but was common parlance at the time when it came to spiritual matters. In Buddhist terminology it might be the 'first state of absorption'.

Here's a note of warning: certain side-effects cannot be ruled out, even if the health consequences of enjoying art, as we have seen, are scientifically disputed. But art and archaeology have a lot to do with pain, loss, death and violence, just like our personal histories. In Pompeii, the city that was 'buried alive' by Vesuvius in 79 CE, this can be felt more clearly than elsewhere.

RISKS AND SIDE-EFFECTS

When I contemplate the plaster casts of children killed in the catastrophe, even after many years in archaeology, for which such objects are 'treasure troves', the academic in me switches off. A five-year-old boy, hit by a 200-degree wave of dust and ash, after eighteen hours of pumice rain and darkness, speaks to the deeply rooted fear of the child in me: the fear of being abandoned in my hour of greatest need. Mummy and Daddy couldn't do any more; they were fighting to save their own lives.

On the other hand, no academic description can capture the moment of happiness when Christopher Clark, in Pompeii to film a documentary, and I stumbled over the small sculpture of a young fisherman asleep. Because his hooded coat is so short he has curled himself up to keep warm, as my eight-year-old son sometimes does. His water jug has toppled over and a rat is nibbling away at something inside his basket on the ground. In the middle of the filming routine it was like a greeting from our inner sun child. On the spur of the moment we decided to include the sculpture in the documentary.

I recall two sentences from Stendhal's description of his Florentine experience, which say far more than the oft-cited heart-thumping and giddiness he felt on his way out of the church: '. . . it all speaks vividly to my soul! Ah! If only I could forget!'[5]

Why forget? I don't know for sure, but I suspect it means that this sort of experience isn't collectable and can't be filed away. Nor can you plan it like a restaurant visit. But, most of all, that our prior knowledge is more of a hindrance than a help, and that it's better forgotten for the moment in question. Such an encounter, between you and the artwork, happens in that moment and then it's over. What remains isn't definable knowledge, it's not a tick on the to-do list, but merely a fleeting escape from the prison of the present. Objects and artworks created hundreds or even thousands of years ago suddenly speak to us – if we listen. The group of 'spiritual pilgrims' include those who visit museums to listen in this way, and thereby risk developing Stendhal syndrome.

All of us are able to join this group. From the standpoint of psychologists who focus on museums, it's quite simple: try it for yourself. If you go to a museum, imagine somebody doing a survey and asking what you're expecting from your visit. Your answer: That it will speak to my soul!

It's not that simple, of course. Maybe the psychology student handing out the questionnaires won't understand the literary reference and will think you're an uncooperative sort, just trying to be funny. That's why I wrote this book. It begins where I believe the root of the problem lies. Those who make pilgrimages to cultural sites need an engine to drive them on. Something to attract them, just as Stendhal was attracted to Italy, the land he kept returning to.

Everyone has such an engine, but I admit that we archaeologists and art historians do little to crank it up. In truth, we are often unsure about what gives us the energy to study broken amphorae or fragments of inscriptions year in, year out. And so we drift into the mere accumulation of factual knowledge and references. It should come as a surprise to no one, therefore, if the public gets bogged down in collecting too.

Take the following scenario. A young person enrols at the department of archaeology in the hope that 'everything will speak vividly to their soul'. At the university there is no talk of soul, however. Instead it's all about collecting: study credits, certificates and catalogues. In archaeology we make catalogues of everything: vases, sarcophagi, subjects of paintings, types of buildings, but also nails, bits of iron slag and roof tiles that have been found on digs. Later, at the PhD stage, it's important to accumulate a few publications, because that's crucial for future career prospects. If you make it to the next level, it continues in the same vein. Now external funding becomes essential, i.e. money from the European Union or other institutions for projects with which you can apply for a chair. For when assessing candidates, the amount of external funding they've accumulated is critical.

By this stage, anyone who can still remember the things that 'speak vividly to their soul' will in most cases have learned to keep these to themselves; they're private, unacademic, childish, perhaps a bit embarrassing too. And thus, what was originally the engine is regarded in academia as unimportant or is even hidden: the engine is kept beneath the bonnet, or hood. And so we teach successive generations to accumulate publications and external funding, and to devise projects for academic exhibitions and museums, without paying much thought to feelings, let alone heavenly ones.

OK, I realise that all of this is a bit exaggerated and no doubt slightly unfair too. I had some fantastic teachers who gave me plenty of inspiration, openness and soul. But that wasn't the mainstream; anyone who does things differently often finds themselves swimming against the tide.

Explaining a work of art, an ancient city or an entire culture is like planting a seed. You can perfect the technique of sowing, you can water, fertilise, tend and nurture. But it needs something else to succeed: fertile ground. The fertile ground is your audience's capacity to let this seed grow. Without that, all efforts are useless. In the science of communicating art (museology) the fertile ground is usually seen as something beyond our control. We try to configure everything possible, from the lighting to the captions, but we take the visitors as they are. Just like businesses take their customers as a given. And that's what they are. No museum or archaeological park should ever consider selecting its public. Everyone is welcome.

We need to begin with ourselves. That's why I've decided in this book to lift the lid. Using Pompeii as an example, I will explain what spurs on an archaeologist like me to devote myself to this place with my heart and soul – from the lavatories (no joke, we've had dissatisfied visitors who've written to the minister of culture on this very topic) to the most recent excavations that continue to add new and occasionally surprising angles to our view of the ancient city.

What this book is about is nothing new, by the way. It's just that experts rarely talk about it among themselves. Seen from the

RISKS AND SIDE-EFFECTS

outside, it's astonishing how seldom in universities and museums the objective pseudo-surface is broken to reveal what drives us emotionally, what 'speaks to our soul'. Obviously this won't find its way into project proposals or specialist publications, but the fact that colleagues rarely discuss it is a bit strange. After all, we're not talking about quantum mechanics here, but human communication and experience, because art history and archaeology are about nothing else.

In itself, the floorplan of a temple is of no interest whatsoever if it doesn't help reconstruct the aesthetic, religious, social and emotional experience that the builders and architects were trying to convey. Seen from this angle, there is a world in every building. And the point of reconstructing this world is to broaden our own world a little, maybe even to put it into perspective; another world is possible, change is possible. Things have transformed, sometimes radically, and will do so in the future too.

Despite this, there are all manner of specialist books full of temple floorplans, but which neglect to mention the world of experience pertaining to these buildings. And surprisingly, there are also authors of such books who would never enquire about their own emotional response to a temple, or that of visitors in antiquity. As if the mere compilation and comparison of floorplans had a purpose in itself that would be positively approved by some superior accounting authority. The fact that one temple had 6×13 columns and another 6×14 isn't an insight, let alone an academic one; it's just numbers. But it's what you'll read in some guidebooks, even though tourists standing by the temple can count for themselves. It would be more interesting to explain what went on inside these columned buildings, but many people think that's suspiciously speculative.

If you climb the tall steps of an ancient Greek temple, your body will tell you that these buildings weren't made for human dimensions. The threshold to the inner area of the Temple of Neptune in Paestum, built in the fifth century BCE, is 82 centimetres high. Here the architecture conveys in a physically tangible way that it was built on a divine scale. The Greek temple is conceived as a 'house of the deity' who 'lives' inside it. This only became clear to me when, as director of the archaeological park of Paestum, where I worked before moving to Pompeii, I had access to the inner area of the temple. That was back in 2015. The decision was then taken to make the interiors of the temples, which at the time were closed to the public, accessible to visitors – in the case of the temple known as the 'Basilica', people were free to walk around it without any barriers, the first and only instance in a ruin of this kind.

In Pompeii too, every day when I'm not travelling for work I try to spend some time among the 2,000-year-old houses. If this doesn't happen in the course of my working day, because I have a meeting at one of the many restoration sites or a tour, I will take a walk in the evening and get the security guards to open locked houses for a few minutes. On these apparently unproductive, but (or maybe for this reason?) inspiring strolls I often get new ideas, and new perspectives suddenly open up.

During my studies we almost never touched on such things. I arrived at the Humboldt University in Berlin imagining that I'd be among people who shared my enthusiasm for antiquity.

RISKS AND SIDE-EFFECTS

But if they did, most of them hid it really well. In seminars and chats outside of the classroom it was mostly a case of people boasting about their factual knowledge. When the eminent professor of archaeology Luca Giuliani came from Munich to Berlin and re-enacted the statue of the Dying Gaul in a guest lecture – he actually sat on the floor in this pose – to show that the figure's attempt to push himself back up with his right hand is doomed to failure for anatomical–physical reasons that anyone can try out for themselves, it was like an epiphany. All the same, I wrote my final paper on something quite different: latrines and sewage systems in ancient Greek cities. My conclusion was that these didn't exist in the time of classical Greece and that we have to imagine the streets of ancient Athens and other artistic centres as open-air cesspits. The only exceptions to this were the shrines and temples, as the boundary between dirty and clean had a religious basis. Looking back, I can see that I was trying to rebel against a whitewashed picture of classical antiquity. Which means it was a sort of revolt against the establishment, and indeed it wasn't long before I received reactions from some professors who didn't want to hear what I had to say.

But that's not the point. The example merely highlights that emotional drivers have a role in one's choice of subject, one's approach and the reactions. I found it fascinating to imagine the Acropolis preserved by all manner of proscriptions, rules and architectural barriers as an island of purity in a city abounding in filth and stench. One inscription has survived, banning cowpats from the sanctuary; how animals were made to refrain from defecating is unknown. At the time I never talked about what had prompted me to embark on this subject, neither to my tutor nor to anyone else. Many things only became clear in hindsight.

This book investigates why we are interested in antiquity and what antiquity says about us. What makes the archaeological discoveries sometimes reported on in the media significant? To find this out we must allow ourselves to get in touch with our personal stories and emotional drivers. Without these there would be no archaeology, no art history or even history; they simply wouldn't make any sense. Stendhal knew this and deep down all of us know it too. We just have to understand that the past has at least as much to do with our own challenges and influences. We must realise that we're the product of the past, the decisions people have taken, sometimes centuries ago, but also that the decisions we make about telling history in a particular way construct the present and the future. Seen this way, the past isn't finished. We, who keep telling and discovering the past, are in the middle of it. *Interbeing*, we could call it, after the Zen Buddhist monk and teacher Thich Nhat Hanh. There's no sure formula for this, but I'll try to explain it using my work in Pompeii as an example. Here's a clue: it's got nothing to do with the number of columns.

CHAPTER ONE
WHAT IS IT ABOUT CLASSICAL ART?

'Do they really mean me?' was one of the many questions that shot through my mind when, one rainy afternoon in February 2021, the phone rang in my office in Paestum and on the line was the Italian ministry of culture. The previous week I'd been one of ten candidates in Rome presenting my ideas for running Pompeii to the selection panel. That was a Thursday. After the interviews the panel had submitted three names to the culture minister, who would have the final say over the appointment. But this is a strictly secret process; you only find out afterwards who made it to the last round. Nonetheless my heart started pounding when the call came. Rejections don't usually come by phone, but in a friendly email wishing you all the best for your future career. The conversation was fairly short. 'I appoint you director of Pompeii,' the minister said, adding that I'd be able to count on the support of the ministry. And something else: not a word to anybody until the official presentation three days later in the Colosseum in Rome.

After hanging up (I'd said: *farò del mio meglio*, 'I'll do my best') I felt giddy. I went outside to the temple ruins in Paestum where it was already getting dark. Pompeii! For classical archaeology (i.e. the archaeology that deals with ancient Greece and Rome) this is roughly the equivalent of the Vatican for the Catholic Church. A place that had played a crucial role in developing modern archaeology and excavation techniques. But also an extremely fragile place. Two-thousand-year-old walls, whose builders could never have dreamed that they'd still be standing today, many covered with stucco and frescoes that – like modern wallpaper – were renewed according to the current fashion. All of this is subject to the weather and streams of tourists, some parts for more than 200 years (the excavations in Pompeii began in 1748). Pompeii thus presents a huge challenge for heritage conservation, a responsibility that is passed from generation to generation like a delicate heirloom that needs protecting.

Most of all, however, Pompeii offers us a unique profile of a provincial city in the ancient Roman world. With its houses, shops, bakeries, brothels, pubs, fountains, squares, temples and cemeteries (which in antiquity always lay outside the city walls) Pompeii is an immeasurably rich source for archaeology.

What is exceptional about Pompeii is that we find things such as statues, paintings, domestic and temple architecture, as well as simple everyday objects, in their ancient context and not, as is usually the case, in so-called secondary contexts. 'Secondary' is the archaeological context of an object when it's no longer where it belongs after use, either because it was thrown away or because after the abandonment of a settlement, 'post-depositional processes' such as weather, decay, flooding or construction work have meant that many centuries later the excavators are presented with a rather confusing picture. A cooking pot, for example, belongs either on a stove or a kitchen shelf. Most pots, however, which in antiquity were often ceramic because metal was expensive and difficult to work, are not excavated from kitchens, but found as shards on rubbish heaps or as infill along with all manner of refuse.

In Pompeii, by contrast, excavations have actually uncovered a whole host of pots on stoves, loaves in ovens, coins in tills and even unmade beds in bedrooms. In archaeology this is sometimes referred to as the 'Pompeii Effect'. On the day that Mount Vesuvius erupted the city was frozen, so to speak, offering a unique opportunity for modern archaeology to plunge into the ancient world.

My doubts as to whether the minister was sure he'd picked the right candidate probably stemmed from the fact that, if I'm being honest, the 'classical' part of classical antiquity has never really interested me. 'What's somebody like that doing in Pompeii?' you may ask. After all, alongside Athens and Rome, it is the UNESCO site where classical antiquity isn't just present but positively celebrated. This book might provide an answer, but one that cannot be clear and unequivocal because our relationship to classical tradition is in many ways double-edged, similar to that between parents and children. We owe it a great deal, but it has also burdened us with much that we'll be trying to rid ourselves of for a long time yet. And like the parent–child relationship, our connection to the 'classical' tends to be emotional. I'm no exception in this regard. This is probably because, even as a child, I felt that a 'classical education' was less of a selfless search for truth and beauty, and more a social exclusion mechanism. You have to be able to afford such an education: piano lessons, family trips to places like Pompeii, Athens or Paris, university ... What's more, does anyone seriously believe that selection in various school systems is purely objective, based on the abilities and achievement of pupils? It's still the case that more children of graduates attend selective schools, whereas children from so-called educationally disadvantaged families are more likely to go to non-selective ones.

I myself went to a German *Gymnasium* (the most academic level of secondary education) and, yes, had piano lessons for a few years with my father, who earned his living as a piano teacher. But for a child of divorced parents in rural Upper Swabia – mother a nurse, father an 'artist' (very suspicious) – a classical education was above all something that subliminally seemed to govern access to the world of 'respectable people'.

In our village we were one of the first families with divorced parents. As our mother didn't come home from work until the afternoon, public-spirited parents of our schoolfriends invited my sister and me to lunch on certain weekdays. We would sit there shyly with the 'respectable people' from whom we were separated by an invisible social divide (a culinary one too: in the kitchen my mother wasn't a patch on the Swabian housewives, of course). We children realised, however, that there was a possibility of securing approval, and that was through 'culture'.

WHAT IS IT ABOUT CLASSICAL ART?

When I played something on the piano or, even better, accompanied the church choir, teachers and parents thought that was great. And when I buckled down at school I could hope that our mother, who was permanently worried about our finances, could come home beaming from parents' evening and say: I'm so proud of you! When parents of my fellow pupils paid me to give Latin coaching, one paterfamilias, who was on the board of a charitable foundation, tapped me on the shoulder and called me 'Herr Professor'. He probably imagined that an academic career might be my point of entry into 'polite society'.

My embracing a classical education and classical music was in many ways linked to our family circumstances rather than to art in the noble sense of the word. Of course, I wasn't fully aware of this at the time and these weren't the only reasons that motivated me to read the 'classics', play the piano or learn Latin. There was something else, a revolutionary, transformational potential of 'classical' art, but I didn't realise this until much later. For a long time classical culture seemed to be an educational canon prescribed from on high, which one simply had to engage with. Beethoven was a must, though blues was more fun. And what was dreamy about Schumann's *Träumerei* (Dreaming), which I encountered in piano lessons? To my mind it was as stuffy as the geraniums on my godmother's balcony. Compared to Laozi, I found Socrates boring and his endless questioning irritating. Instead of burying myself in Gustav Schwab's *Sagen des klassischen Altertums* ('Legends of the Classical Age'), which stood on my mother's bookshelf, I preferred to read the myths of the indigenous peoples of North America. Few works of art seemed to be as meaningless as the

THE BURIED CITY

Apollo Belvedere, which Johann Joachim Winckelmann, the founder of classical archaeology, hyped in the eighteenth century as the ideal of classical beauty. I was baffled by what was supposed to be beautiful, let alone moving, about a naked man in sandals, who reminded me of the naturists on the beach I found so embarrassing. On our school trip to Rome I preferred exploring the winding ghetto, the mediaeval Jewish quarter on the banks of the Tiber, than the ancient Forum Romanum, which came across as disappointingly small and straightforward. And much more fascinating to me than a classical temple in all its symmetry and transparency were the old farmhouses crouched on the Upper Swabian hills, in which centuries-old secrets seemed to lie dormant. A far cry from the urban residences of Pompeii with their colourful stucco, imitating Greek marble and preserved in all colours and shades thanks to the 'Pompeii Effect'. Or maybe not? Are the two actually closer than they appear?

How does the Pompeii Effect come about? How precisely do we have to imagine the eruption of Mount Vesuvius, which preserved for us so incomparably a city in the classical world, including loaves in ovens and pots on stoves? This question is not that simple to answer.

On the one hand we are helped by ancient text sources, especially two letters that Pliny the Younger wrote to the historian

WHAT IS IT ABOUT CLASSICAL ART?

Tacitus. In these he described how his uncle, Pliny the Elder, a naval commander stationed in Misenum (to the west of Naples), set sail in a ship, initially to watch the natural spectacle at close quarters (besides being a high-ranking Roman official, Pliny's uncle was also a passionate researcher whose thirty-seven-volume *Natural History* has survived). Then, when he realised the seriousness of the situation, he sought to help the people in distress, dying himself during the disaster. Overweight and with breathing difficulties, he took his last gasp on the beach of Stabiae, not far from Pompeii, where he was trying to escape by boat with friends, which was thwarted by the sea swells caused by the volcanic eruption. When, as his nephew Pliny the Younger says, the general's body was found on the 'third day' after the beginning of the catastrophe, he appeared 'intact . . . looking like a sleeping man rather than a dead one'.[6] These days we would say 'two days later' rather than 'on the third day'. The ancient Romans and Greeks always included the first day when they counted, which is why it says in the New Testament that Jesus rose from the dead on the third day, i.e. the Sunday after Good Friday.

On the other hand we are helped by vulcanology, the science of volcanic eruptions. Like archaeologists, vulcanologists also dig around in the layers of ash and lapilli (small pumice stones) around Vesuvius, occasionally leading to friction and (purely academic) tussles, but all in all both sides end up hugely enriched. Whereas archaeologists are mainly interested in what the burial of Pompeii says about the situation directly prior to the disaster, vulcanologists dig in the ashes and stones to understand the precise dynamics of the eruption itself.

THE BURIED CITY

In recent years when, thanks to a major Italian–European project, large-scale excavations have taken place in Pompeii for the first time in a long while, it's become increasingly clear that very different circumstances prevailed depending on the distance from Vesuvius and the local conditions. Today we can reconstruct the sequence of events for Pompeii roughly as follows.[7]

The hell, which would end in the total destruction of the city and the death of many of its inhabitants, was unleashed in the late morning of an autumn day in 79 CE. It took a long time for those in the firing line to realise what was actually happening. It must be noted that Mount Vesuvius looked very different before the eruption in 79 CE. It didn't have the typical conical form of a volcano that we see today, but appeared as a massif with a relatively flat summit, apart from a few rocky outcrops from the wooded landscape, which played a role in the Spartacus Revolt from 73 to 71 BCE (but that's another story). The reason for this is that the volcano hadn't erupted for almost 300 years. The last occasion had been in 217 BCE, but even a few generations after this most historians knew nothing about it. In 79 CE, nobody anticipated the deadly danger lurking beneath the earth's crust. During those long years of forgetting, a huge amount of energy had accumulated underground that eventually burst forth.[8]

The top of the mountain literally exploded; the magma that shot up from the bowels of the earth blasted with great force the 'plug' of stone and mud into the air, which had blocked its path upwards. A cloud of 'unusual size and form' took shape, which Pliny compared to a pine tree; nowadays it might remind us more of an atomic mushroom cloud. Ash, flowing magma and stones towered to a height of 32 kilometres, that's to say into the stratosphere, the second layer of the geosphere, of which the ozone layer is also a part.

Soon it began to rain small pumice stones, so-called lapilli. The wind was not in Pompeii's favour, driving the stony rain from the eruption cloud southwards, where the city lay not far from the mouth of the River Sarno, unprepared for what was to come.

Instinctively most people did what I imagine anyone would do when it's raining stones: they sought shelter in houses or the porticos that lined the streets, squares and courtyards. Although lapilli aren't particularly big, between the size of a pea and a walnut, flying among them were 'bombs', larger lava stones that could seriously injure or even kill people.

As obvious as it might seem, taking shelter proved to be a deadly trap for many. For the stone rain was to last between eighteen and nineteen hours, through to the morning of the following day. The layer of lapilli grew by about 15 centimetres per hour, covering streets, fields, squares and roofs. In eighteen hours that equates to more than 2.5 metres. Many roofs collapsed beneath the weight. It has been calculated that the weight bearing down on each square metre of roof increased by 100 kilogrammes per hour. But even where roofs held firm, people were soon in danger of not being able to leave the rooms they'd sought refuge in because the lapilli had buried windows and doors.

Worse was to come. After almost twenty hours in which the mushroom-shaped cloud had soared upwards, it now began to implode. You can get an idea of what happened by aiming a garden hose vertically upwards then turning off the tap. The column of pumice and ash that had formed above Vesuvius didn't collapse all at once, however, but bit by bit until the entire tower eventually came crashing down. This produced pyroclastic waves that radiated outwards from the base of the column at speeds of up to 100 kilometres per hour. When tower blocks are demolished you sometimes see similar pressure waves of dust, only that in this case our tower block was 32 kilometres high. The force of these waves was enormous. And they were extremely hot, around 200–300 degrees Celsius.

The first of the waves, the result of the still incomplete collapse of the column, was halted by the ancient stone wall of Pompeii. That must have been early in the morning of day two of the catastrophe. Two further waves followed, which cleared the wall, but had exhausted most of their destructive power between the volcano and the city. The fourth wave was the most devastating, reaching Pompeii between seven and eight in the morning. Parts of buildings that still projected from the 3-metre-tall layers of lapilli were swept away. People and animals died from heat shock or suffocation. Internal spaces that had remained free from lapilli were filled with hot ash dust, which enveloped people and animals as well as furnishings. Meanwhile, those who at the break of day had decided to escape over the heaps of lapilli, perhaps with a cushion tied to their head – like Pliny according to his nephew's account – were decimated. The escapees couldn't see much anyway, as the eruption had almost completely darkened the sky. 'Many people beseeched the gods,' Pliny the Younger writes, witnessing the eruption from Misenum. 'Others said there were no longer any gods and an eternal new darkness had burst forth into the world.'[9]

'On Sunday we were in Pompeii,' Goethe noted on 13 March 1787 in his *Italian Journey*. 'There has been much calamity in the world, but little that has given so much pleasure to posterity.'[10] But can we really take pleasure in such suffering? The more we learn about the catastrophe, the harder it is to come up with a clear answer.

Being able to work in Pompeii is a privilege. But the disaster is ubiquitous. In daily life it recedes behind construction site appointments, discussions, video conferences, board meetings and staff association meetings. But it's never completely gone. In 2015, when I was working on the EU and government-funded 'Great Pompeii Project' to improve the conservation of the site after years of neglect and decay, I met a colleague who was particularly sensitive to this. In her work as an architect she had visions of the ancient inhabitants, sitting in the streets, heads in hands.

At any rate the delight must have been palpable when, on 8 November 1853, an unusually beautiful statue of the god Apollo emerged from the lapilli. It might not have been the Apollo Belvedere, but a work of similar importance that gave the name to the house in which it was found: House of the Citharist or the 'house of the kithara-playing Apollo' (the kithara is a sort of lyre and from this Greek word comes our 'guitar'). The statue is pictured in many handbooks of ancient Greek art.

You have to read between the lines of the sober diary entry of the excavators to guess at the excitement over this significant find:

> It was unearthed around two o'clock in the afternoon on the floor of the peristyle of the house on the corner of so-called Via Stabiana and the road to the amphitheatre, whose entrance is marked number 110. Bronze. A statue of a male nude on a round base. The hair is tied to the forehead with a band and falls in two curls on either side to the shoulders and top of the chest. The right arm hangs down by the hip, the corresponding hand holding a plectrum, while the left arm is raised to the chest and in the corresponding hand a small plate was fixed with a square hole in which a lyre or other musical instrument could be mounted, which has not yet been found.[11]

The instrument is still missing. Despite the Pompeii Effect, there are gaps in the documentation for which there could be a variety of explanations. After the eruption many people came back to dig for their belongings in the moonscape that had replaced the city. The forum, the ancient main square that boasted honorific statues and marble cladding, was in fact systematically plundered. But some gaps go back to ancient repair works. In 62 CE Pompeii was struck by a serious earthquake, and so in many places they were still patching up and renovating in 79 CE. In the course of these works statues were moved and in some cases revamped.

Today we know that the earthquake of 62 CE was a harbinger of the volcanic eruption seventeen years later. Beneath the earth the magma was rumbling. The ancient inhabitants of Pompeii had no idea about this, however. They rebuilt their city with confidence and much hard work.

But what does the statue have to do with 'Greek' art? After all, it was found in a Roman house in Italy.

We must not forget that the Romans had their 'classical age' too. These days Cicero and Ovid are set texts at school, but they weren't in their own day; they were as contemporary as Zadie Smith or Noam Chomsky are now. What's more, both Cicero and Ovid met a sad, not particularly classical, end. During the civil war (49–45 BCE) Cicero ended up on a proscription list, that's to say a list of 'outlawed' state enemies who were simply slaughtered. Ovid was banished, no doubt having versified too candidly. He'd also gone on benders with the daughter of Emperor Augustus, if not worse.

For the ancient Romans, whom we regard as belonging to classical antiquity, the 'classical age' was Greek culture of the fifth and fourth centuries BCE. Just as today we learn Latin, French and Spanish, they learned Greek. In Pompeii there are a number of inscriptions and graffiti in Greek, some clearly written by schoolchildren labouring over Greek grammar.

What today appears as the whole of the culture of antiquity was thus divided into classical and less classical, contemporary and time-honoured. We must, therefore, talk of the classical in the plural; what is classical is always in the eye of the beholder. Every generation defines for itself what it deems to be classical. Sometimes it might be just a slight shift, at other times a radical reinterpretation. The Renaissance and Neoclassicism are two such major reinterpretations that suddenly call everything into question, deriving quite different, sometimes revolutionary values from what is seemingly familiar. Finally, modernity made an ideal of the anti-classical, but even reversal and rejection keep the classical as an influential point of reference. Somehow the anti-classical always brings us back to the classical; maybe that's why they say that all roads lead to Rome.

When in 2001 I enrolled at the Humboldt University in Berlin to study Classical Archaeology and Ancient Greek, it was because I was fascinated by the nature of everyday life in the remote past. How did people live, how did migration, trade and communication work in an age when there were no dictionaries, nautical charts or steamboats, let alone telephone or internet? As I've said, I found statues and temples rather boring. This changed when I attended a seminar on the classicism of the imperial Roman age, to which the bronze Apollo from Pompeii belongs. Because of their veneration of Greek classicism, the Romans decorated their temples and houses with Greek works of art. This led to serious looting in Greece – art theft was already around in antiquity. Letters written by Cicero to his friend Atticus, who was staying in Greece, read like orders from an art dealer: 'I'm waiting with great anticipation for the Megarian statues and herms you told me about. Don't hesitate to send whatever you've got of the same sort and what you think is worthy of the "Academy"; you can trust my purse. That's what I want; I need everything that's suitable for a "Gymnasium".[12]

'Herms' are traditional Greek busts on rectangular pillars. 'Academy' and 'Gymnasium' are Greek terms that Cicero used to describe parts of his villa which were based on Greek architectural forms and which he intended to decorate with 'worthy' Greek statues. The peristyle (columned courtyard) in the House of the Citharist where the statue of Apollo was found is one of those elements of private luxury architecture that came from Greece to Italy. In this way Cicero and other members of the upper class created their own miniature Greece in the gardens behind their houses. This wasn't just for their personal relaxation, but to convey to visitors that they understood something of classical culture, unlike the proletariat and nouveaux-riches, who lacked the means or necessary education. This is classical antiquity as a marker of social distinction, even though classical antiquity, from our perspective at least, hadn't yet come to an end.

What's fascinating about this is, first, the social function of classical education, which we still encounter today; and, second, the possibility of a creative reinterpretation of the classical – a phenomenon that likewise has parallels in later eras.

The statue of Apollo the Citharist is an imitation of a Greek sculpture from the mid-fifth century BCE. The original was probably made for a temple, as in the Greek classical age exhibiting such works in a private house was unthinkable. Statues of gods had the function of recalling the presence of the deity. These were deeply religious works where the artistic aspect was of secondary importance. Apollo is the god of medicine, music and harmony, which is why he is often depicted with a lyre or kithara. He 'leads the muses in their round dance', presides over musical and sporting competitions, for example in Delphi, his most important temple. He is sporty and young; unlike Zeus or Poseidon, he's portrayed without a beard and with long hair.

But he has his dark side too. Not only does he absolve matricides like Orestes of Mycenae, 'cleansing' them of the blood they have stained themselves with, to restore the harmony that is so dear to his heart, he is himself a murderer. Together with his twin sister Artemis he killed all of Niobe's fourteen children, after she'd boasted of having more offspring than Apollo's mother. This is how the twins are depicted in the Sanctuary of Apollo in Pompeii. Apollo and Artemis with bow and arrow, the weapons of the divine siblings, stand opposite each other as statues outside the temple.

To found his world-famous temple in Delphi, to which even princes from non-Greek, 'barbarian' lands paid pilgrimage, Apollo killed Python, the dragon who'd owned the site of the temple beforehand. Afterwards he, the healer, had to have himself cleansed of this blood guilt because, according to the ancient Greeks, nobody is able to absolve themselves.

WHAT IS IT ABOUT CLASSICAL ART?

Anybody keen to avoid Apollo's revenge did well to consult his oracle in Delphi. There, the Pythia, a priestess who prophesied in a sort of trance, would answer the petitioner, albeit often in puzzling sayings that could easily be misunderstood. To Croesus, the king of Lydia who was seeking advice in Delphi about a planned campaign against the mighty Persian Empire, she answered, 'You will destroy a great empire.'

Croesus attacked, only to realise too late that the empire he was destroying was his own. This is no legend; Croesus really existed and the war between Lydia and Persia did actually take place. We even know the year it broke out: 547 BCE. Of course, nobody can verify what the Pythia murmured to the king in the dim light of the temple, enveloped in heady vapours that apparently rose from a crack in the rocks inside the temple. Nor can we know if clever priests reinterpreted her babbled answer, either on the spot or afterwards, to preserve the temple's reputation.

Another of Apollo's dark sides is that the god of medicine is also the one who sends down plague and illness. This never happens arbitrarily, however, but to expose a hidden or hushed-up grievance. When, for example, Oedipus unwittingly marries his mother and rules as king in Thebes, Apollo afflicts the city with a pestilence until the incest comes to light. In the fifth century BCE the tragedian Sophocles brilliantly dramatised how the unaware Oedipus conducts investigations, at the end of which it turns out that he himself is the reason for the plague, as he killed his father and slept with his mother.

In fairness we ought to point out that Oedipus's parents abandoned him as a newborn baby in the wilderness, the reason for this being once again an oracle. According to the prophecy, the child would kill his father, which of course happened despite – or rather because of – his being abandoned. A shepherd found the helpless baby and he was raised by other parents. When Oedipus grew to become a man he killed a stranger in an argument. This stranger was in fact his father.

Anyone wishing to read more into this than the gods cynically toying with clueless people need look no further than a saying engraved on a column at the temple in Delphi: *Gnōthi seauton*, 'Know thyself!' As in the case of Oedipus, Apollo is asking this of us: when looking for the reasons for grievances, disharmony and sickness, we should begin with ourselves. If the Pythia were still soothsaying today, her answer to the COVID-19 pandemic would probably have been along the lines of: Look for the deeper reason; vaccination alone will not suffice . . .

The master of the House of the Citharist who commissioned the statue must have known a thing or two about the Greek god. After all, there is an Apollo temple in Pompeii as well, which counts among the oldest in the city. He was probably able to translate *Gnōthi seauton* into Latin too, which would be *nosce te ipsum*. But the motivation for investing so much money in a bronze statue was unlikely to have been a religious one.

Talking of cost, we mustn't fool ourselves as to the price of copies of Greek originals. Archaeologists estimate that with the

WHAT IS IT ABOUT CLASSICAL ART?

technology available at the time it was about twice as expensive to copy a statue as to create one from scratch. The more accurate the copy, the more costly it became. Specialist instruments were used to take exact measurements of the original and transfer them to the copy.

Whereas the kithara player from Pompeii is a fairly loose imitation of a Greek work, it's no coincidence that the most precise copies are in the most exquisite villas. An emperor such as Hadrian could even allow himself to exhibit two almost identical copies of the statue of a discus thrower by the Greek sculptor Myron in his villa near Tivoli. Here he wasn't just demonstrating his love for Greek art, but the depths of his imperial coffers that permitted such an outlay.

In antiquity, the copy had a completely different value from today, where it's generally regarded as inferior. But this has only been true since modern technology made it possible to produce copies on an industrial scale. As our example shows, what is considered to be high and low quality in art depends on the technology of the time. In this respect we are currently living in an exciting era, as digital technologies such as NFTs (non-fungible tokens) are producing completely new forms of (digital) art.

But what was the houseowner's motivation in Pompeii for displaying such an expensive statue in the garden? Apart from sheer swagger (I can afford it!) the sensuality of the male body played a key role. Often it didn't much matter whether the figure was Apollo or Dionysus, another young god. Much more important, it seemed, was to be surrounded by representations of beautiful bodies. The houses of Pompeii are brimming with sensuality and eroticism. We're not talking primarily about the pornographic images, some crude, that were under lock and key in the notorious 'Secret Cabinet' of the National Archaeological Museum in Naples. The public is now able to view this collection of explicit sexual imagery (one highlight is the god Pan having sex with a goat), but in the nineteenth century it was only accessible to morally upright, mature visitors. In Pompeii too there are pornographic pictures, for example in the Lupanar, the local brothel, where a specific sexual position is depicted above each of the five small rooms where the prostitutes plied their trade. The images all show heterosexual couples, which doesn't mean that there weren't boys and men among the prostitutes too. If so, however, they were clearly in a minority.

The Lupanar, by the way, is one of the most visited places in Pompeii, although to be honest I don't really know what I should think of that. At the beginning of my time as director, when we reopened the Lupanar after a lengthy closure due to the pandemic, I was concerned that a place of extreme sexual exploitation (many of the prostitutes were slaves) would become a salacious tourist attraction, where there was no trace of all the suffering and social inequality. I have to say, however, that I've been surprised by the visitors in a positive way; on my rounds and chance encounters I've noticed that many of them are asking similar questions and, depending on their cultural background, often talk about it openly too.

In the houses of Pompeii, depictions of sex like those in the Lupanar are rare, though they certainly exist. (In these cases some archaeologists doggedly deny that these are homes,

WHAT IS IT ABOUT CLASSICAL ART?

assuming instead that all rooms with such pictures were for prostitution.) On the other hand, sensual and openly erotic imagery is everywhere in Pompeii. Ariadne and Dionysus, Venus and Mars, nymphs and satyrs, Narcissus with his reflection, the goddess of the moon Selene and handsome Endymion who must sleep forever so that Selene can gaze at him – the list of lovers who appear on the walls of Pompeii goes on and on. And it's not restricted to the human race; we also find male and female centaurs.

In 2018 the discovery of a particularly high-quality mural caused a sensation. It depicts an unclothed Leda and a swan about to mate with her. The swan is Zeus in disguise and their union will produce Helen, the most beautiful woman in Greece. She has a human form but hatches from an egg. How that is supposed to work biologically was already a matter of dispute in antiquity.

The walls of Pompeii are also full of Cupids, small, winged boys who represent love: *Eros* in Greek, *Amor* in Latin, both grammatically masculine. Eroticism (the word comes from *Eros*) seems to be what most interested the Romans about the Greek myths. If a mythological wall painting in Pompeii is devoid of erotic content then it's an exception.

This is partly because there is no lack of sex in Greek mythology, but also because the Romans particularly emphasised this aspect in their appropriation of Greek mythological imagery. For eroticism was originally alien to their own culture. The Romans and other peoples of ancient Italy had no mythology comparable to the Greek. Much of what later passed for ancient Roman mythology was concocted later. By the same token the

Romans didn't have an art or literature from the 'good old days' on a par with those of the Greeks.

The Greeks saw the Romans as 'barbarians' who lacked a sense of art, civilisation and erotic finesse. So when in the course of the second century BCE the Romans conquered Greece, the world appeared to have been turned on its head. The Greeks saw themselves as ruled by conquerors whom they believed to be their cultural inferiors, while the Romans worried about being infected, maybe even morally corrupted, by the sophisticated culture of their new subjects. 'Greece, vanquished by the sword, submitted to the coarse victor and brought the arts to uncouth Latium,' Horace wrote in the first century BCE.[13]

Philosophy, drama and literature, painting and sculpture, but also astrology and Dionysian trance rituals – the Romans considered all of these to be Oriental and potential threats to ancient Roman morality.

One of the most controversial topics, however, was male homoeroticism. In classical Greece this had its fixed place in society, albeit governed by strict rules. An erotic relationship between two men was socially acceptable if one was young and the other mature and experienced. The relationship was not just about sex but pedagogy too. The elder gave the younger one an introduction into society: politics, war, sport ... The settings for this were the palaestra, where men took part (naked) in athletic competitions, and the symposium, the drinking party to which only men were allowed access. The women who took part were either dancers or prostitutes. As well as drinking wine at the symposium, the men debated, versified and sang. A number of drinking songs eulogise the beauty of young men, sometimes with unequivocal undertones.

All of this was highly suspect as far as the Romans were concerned, as their culture was based on very different values. For one thing, the Roman banquet had always been open to wives and daughters too, so it wasn't the place for a boys' night out. Also, from a Roman perspective it was abominable for a male citizen to give themselves up for sex with another male citizen, irrespective of age. This is the difference from Greek culture. It doesn't mean that homosexuality wasn't tolerated, but any citizen who sought a same-sex relationship could only conduct one with a non-citizen, i.e. a slave or foreigner, or they risked the loss of their social status. This explains why Cicero on the one hand railed against homosexual colleagues (i.e. Roman citizens), but praised the attractiveness of his private secretary (a slave). Later, in the second century CE, Emperor Hadrian had an official lover: Antinous of Bithynia, in present-day Turkey. It was not by chance that Antinous didn't possess Roman citizenship. Otherwise Hadrian would have been guilty of offending the accepted morality of the time.

Moreover, most men who we know had same-sex relationships were bisexual in the modern sense. They were married and some also had extra-marital affairs with other women. The modern distinction between homosexuality and heterosexuality was completely alien to the ancient world; the corresponding terms didn't even exist. Nobody had to commit themselves to a specific sexual orientation. This only came to an end under Christianity, which defined sexuality as an obstacle to the union with God and thus immoral. From that point on only heterosexual relationships were permitted and these for the sole purpose of procreation.

The modern papal polemic against condoms and contraceptive pills would appear completely incomprehensible to the ancient Romans of the pre-Christian era, who protected themselves with plant substances, by using the rhythm method or through *coitus interruptus*. The same is true of abortion. As it came with such a great risk in antiquity there was an eyewatering number of abandoned newborns, which archaeological excavations of babies' corpses in dried-up fountains and on rubbish heaps attest to. Oedipus's abandonment as a baby was an everyday occurrence and thus familiar to the public of the ancient world. But even if this was a widespread practice, each instance was an individual life associated with unimaginable psychological and physical pain.

In the attempt to introduce the sophistication of the Greek symposium into 'uncouth Latium' without violating the basic norms of Roman tradition, art played an important role. Statues and pictures created a Greek-like ambience in which the classical homoeroticism of Greece was ubiquitous, without it necessarily entailing the adoption of the corresponding practices.

This becomes particularly clear if we look at the *pueri delicati*, the 'delicate boys'. These were teenage slaves trained to wait on the guests at drinking parties and provide sexual services to their masters. To an extent, they assumed the role of the young Greek men at the symposium. Slaves like these were particularly expensive. Often a miserable fate awaited them. Once they'd grown beyond their youth and thus were no longer sexually attractive, these men, without any other education or training, were thrown out onto the street as if they were useless objects to be discarded.

In the House of Marcus Fabius Rufus on the eastern outskirts of Pompeii a statue was found depicting one of these 'delicate boys'. Statues like this were displayed in banqueting rooms as 'silent servants'. In the case of the statue from Pompeii it was a lampstand. The bronze boy in the House of Marcus Fabius Rufus stood naked in the corner, the flickering light of the lamps he held seemingly bringing him to life, especially after a few cups of Campanian wine. The statue is a substitute for a real boy, who in turn is a sort of substitute for the Greek form of homoeroticism that wasn't tolerated in Roman Italy.

And thus the artworks kept circling around the controversial topic of homoeroticism in all its aspects between Greek and Roman tradition, without coming to any clear conclusions. Delicate boy and sexual object, or just a harmless lampstand in the Greek style?

Even greater is the ambivalence in the case of the Apollo the Citharist. After all, the statue represents a god rather than a 'catamite'. Yet it is completely influenced by the aesthetic of a young male body, which developed in the context of classical Greek homoeroticism. This explains why those who could afford them put such statues in their private homes. The reason wasn't religious zeal; the Greek myths and figures of deities were little more than an excuse. This can also be seen in the choice of myths and gods depicted in the houses of Pompeii. The establishment gods such as Jupiter, Juno and Minerva, powerful but not very sexy, appear only as peripheral figures. Dominating the imagery are Apollo, Dionysus and of course

Venus, usually scantily clad or naked. The point here was to show the sheer beauty of the goddess of love, who didn't adhere to the dress code of female Roman citizens (veil and ankle-length skirt), but also to show how beautiful a man could be.

The number of residential units in the area of Pompeii that has been excavated runs to over 1,000. They range from one-room apartments with an integrated shop to luxury urban villas, such as the House of the Faun, which occupies an entire block. Keeping track of everything is difficult; you need to knuckle down when getting involved professionally with this place.

In my case the energy to do this came from the urge to rebel – because what I was taught about Pompeii in lectures and seminars would never have been able to motivate me to work my way from beginning to end through the eleven fat volumes of *Pompei: Pitture e Mosaici* ('Pompeii: Paintings and Mosaics') in my spare time. These tomes contain the complete documentation of the murals and mosaics of Pompeii in black-and-white photographs and detailed descriptions, house by house, room by room. I was searching for depictions of Hermaphroditus, a figure in Greek mythology who combined male and female body parts. In Pompeii there are around twenty such depictions.

When I studied at the Humboldt University someone wrote a PhD on Hermaphroditus in Greek–Roman art at the Institute of Classical Archaeology, entitled *Das Weib im Manne* ('The Woman in the Man'). The author came to the conclusion that Hermaphroditus was an artistic creation who had nothing to do with real sexuality or hermaphroditism.

I found this interpretation of Hermaphroditus intuitively wrong. In retrospect I think what bothered me was the separation between art and social reality. It was as if the thesis was trying to say: We can talk about Hermaphroditus as a fictional character without touching on difficult and uncomfortable topics such as genderfluidity and sexuality. This was in 2005, at a time when Gender Studies was a relatively new discipline. Most professors, especially in a naturally conservative subject like archaeology, made no secret of their rejection of this novel development, although they hid their criticism behind spiteful jibes that were supposed to be funny but which I found cringe-worthy. Maybe 'depressing' describes it more accurately; it was depressing, I thought, that in the big city and at such an august institution as the Humboldt, which prided itself on its Enlightenment values, there was a place for prejudice and macho leg-pulling. Which is precisely what I'd wanted to escape from. But the city was in danger of turning out to be the continuation of the village by other means.

I went in search of like-minded people and eventually we set up a student working group on Hermaphroditus, for which the name 'Hermi' stuck. The subject hasn't left me since, even though I've dealt with completely different ones in the meantime. My first Pompeii exhibition, which I curated together with the Italian archaeologist Maria Luisa Catoni, was on 'Art and Sensuality in the Houses of Pompeii'. My article in the exhibition catalogue was on hermaphrodites and centaurs. I emailed my former working group with the words: 'Hermi's march through the institutions!'

Most of the group are working in other fields today, and I barely have contact with some of them. But I will be eternally grateful to each and every one for an experience that taught me more than most of the lectures and seminars on my timetable.

The heart of our group was Matthias Mergl. When I met him I was in my first semester; he in his thirteenth. When I did my PhD he was still studying. From a village in Upper Franconia, Matthias trained as a medical orderly before studying Classical Archaeology because he 'wanted to understand how everything really hangs together'. He also studied Pre- and Protohistory, Gender Studies and Scandinavian Studies (all as main subjects), learned ancient Greek, Norwegian and Icelandic, and worked in a library. Now he's back working in healthcare, part-time so he can dedicate the rest of his time to his research. Despite this, or perhaps because of it, he is to my mind a greater 'scholar' than many esteemed professors who diligently publish one article after another, but essentially have lost their passion for academic study.

Sometimes I say in jest that I studied under Matthias Mergl, but there is a hint of truth in this. We would sit for hours in cafés or at his place in Oranienstrasse, discussing gender studies or French poststructuralists. Through him I met people with completely different interests, for example his partner Wolfgang Müller, who in the 1980s was a member of the punk band Die tödliche Doris ('Deadly Doris') and included elves in his performances. Or Natalie Nagel, who studied literature and speculated about things like gendered violence in the novels of Adalbert Stifter (now she's Professor of German Literature in Princeton). In the evenings we often met in a bar at Kottbusser Tor. On the roof of the 1970s prefabricated building was an illuminated advertisement for 'Möbel Olfe' ('Olfe Furniture') in huge letters, even though the shop no longer existed. The bar had simply adopted the name. So the city wasn't a continuation of the village by other means after all.

On those evenings I encountered perspectives that put a whole new complexion on what I was learning on my archaeology course. Maybe that sounds a bit excessive, but routine in academia shouldn't be underestimated. Especially in Classical Studies (Archaeology, Ancient Greek, Latin and Ancient History) there was a tendency among academics at the time to shut themselves away. Classical Studies suffered (and still suffers) enormously from a loss of importance as a result of the decline in the middle-class humanist educational ideal. The time when Latin was learned before modern foreign languages and when classical art was an unchallenged ideal is over. Academics who study classical antiquity are no longer afforded the social recognition and media attention they automatically enjoyed in the nineteenth and early twentieth centuries. Instead of going on the offensive and confronting this radical change with creativity, many in the discipline have withdrawn into their own worlds. And so Classical Archaeology, once the leading light in all manner of innovations, now limps behind the other humanities.

This is something we also felt in our working group. In the end we managed to offer a student seminar. We didn't award marks, of course, but those attending the seminar were able to include the hours in their study record. But it took a long time to get there. I still recall a plenary session of members of the university's August Boeckh Centre for Antiquity (not a particularly appealing name, I know, but the official abbreviation ABAZ seems little better to me) at which we were to present our project to the professors.

Our methodological approach was based on the work of Michel Foucault, who founded discourse analysis in France in the 1970s and 1980s. Put very simply, this argues that *what* we say cannot be divorced from *where, how* and *in what function* we say it. An example from Foucault's own research is medicine, which didn't always determine who is mentally healthy ('normal') and who is mentally ill ('mad'), but only acquired this authority that holds sway over freedom and unfreedom, sometimes even over life and death, in the course of the nineteenth century.

In a similar way we wanted to investigate what the pictures of Hermaphroditus said about ancient bodily ideals and norms. Discourse analysis had long been part of everyday academic life in other disciplines. In the August Boeckh Centre for Antiquity, by contrast, one professor of Church History felt obliged to say that we ought to avoid using the term 'discourse'. It was just a buzzword, he said, which would vanish as quickly as it had appeared. Besides, he added, Foucault was already passé.

Michel Foucault died of Aids in 1984 and nowadays is regarded as a major figure of European intellectual history. In his multi-volume work *The History of Sexuality* he also looked

WHAT IS IT ABOUT CLASSICAL ART?

at antiquity. At some point, hopefully, this will be perceived by the mainstream as an inspiring addition to Classical Studies rather than a disruptive fad.

The question of 'how' in discursive analysis helps us break free from the illusion that the meaning and content of a statement necessarily coincide. Deep down we're all aware of this from practical experience in our lives. Anyone who lives in a relationship knows, for example, that the question 'What did you do today?' can be asked in a thousand different ways, from lovingly interested to reproachfully aggressive. It all depends on the tone, body language, situation, background.

What's lacking is the translation of this practical experience into academic research. Western thought is very strongly 'logocentric', that's to say we assume there is an absolute, unshakable truth ('content') behind shells of words and changing modes of expression ('form'). Discourse analysis doesn't mean, as its critics sometimes claim, doubting the possibility of truth per se and thus relativising everything. It's far more about making clear that we only ever get the truth packaged up, and the packaging consists of words and texts, as well as images, gestures, archives, schooling or patterns of thought.

In our working group we wanted to look at how Hermaphroditus was 'packaged' in Pompeii. How did these images of the Greek mythical figure fit into the everyday lives of the inhabitants of

Pompeii? In which rooms and setting is Hermaphroditus depicted, and what does this tell us about his significance?

The findings didn't come close to what I'd expected. I'd thought that this figure was a feminised male body, and thus Hermaphroditus would be an extreme form of the graceful, slightly feminine-looking ideal of beauty that we've already seen in the classical statue of Apollo the Citharist. This reading tallies with the *content* of the myth (beware logocentrism!). In Ovid's *Metamorphoses* Hermaphroditus is a young man who gets into a pool, where he is turned into a 'half man' by the nymph Salmacis, whose love he has rejected. When the nymph blends into his body, her identity disappears, while female breasts and features appear on Hermaphroditus's body.

The problem is that this story doesn't correspond at all to the 'packaging' of Hermaphroditus in Pompeii. By packaging we mean the way in which Hermaphroditus appears in the pictures. A note of caution here: we are not trying to claim that the content is totally different. There is no doubt that the pictures portray Hermaphroditus. But they do this in a way that is in stark contrast to the myth as passed down by the poet Ovid. Time and again the images tell a very different story, that of a woman changing into a man. What's being depicted visually isn't a 'woman in the man' but a 'man in the woman'. A painted room in Pompeii's House of the Vettii illustrates this particularly well.

WHAT IS IT ABOUT CLASSICAL ART?

The Vettii were two slaves who'd been freed, something that happened often in the imperial Roman era.[14] The hope of a free life was supposed to encourage a slave to serve their master faithfully, seeing as he was the only person who could decide to set them free. But as the years passed a slave also risked becoming a burden on their master. The slaveowner was in danger of having to provide for ageing slaves even though they were barely making a contribution to the housework anymore. Releasing a slave was a double-edged sword, therefore. If it went badly, those set free, *liberti* in Latin, were granted a freedom that could mean homelessness and dying of hunger. In such a case 'freedom' meant no longer having a master who supported you. Some freed slaves, on the other hand, managed to make a living and a few of them even amassed considerable wealth for which many a freeborn man envied them. In this category were the Vettii: Aulus Vettius Conviva and Aulus Vettius Restitutus. They probably acquired part of their fortune from the wine trade, which played a significant role in Pompeii, even though the city's plonk was considered to be inferior. 'Traveller, eat the bread in Pompeii but drink the wine in Nocera' (a neighbouring city) was the advice scrawled on a wall.[15]

Although the House of the Vettii wasn't one of the largest in Pompeii it wasn't particularly small either and was richly decorated with paintings and sculptures. The social climbers clearly weren't shy about showing off their newly acquired wealth.

After the earthquake of 62 CE the murals in the House of the Vettii were almost completely restored. They are thus among the most impressive examples of the 'fourth style'. This fourth style denotes the last phase of Pompeian wall painting.

Remnants of the three older styles can be found scattered around the rest of the city.

In the nineteenth century the German archaeologist August Mau (the only non-Italian to have been accorded a bust in the portrait gallery of important researchers and directors on the terrace in front of Pompeii's 'Antiquarium') noticed that the different styles of wall painting in Pompeii came from different eras. The fourth style had come into fashion around 50 CE and was dominant by the time Vesuvius erupted in 79 CE. It's characterised by the depiction of myths that are resplendent in the middle of the walls like painted panels, whereas the sides and upper areas of the walls are filled with stunning trompe l'oeil architecture.

Before the fourth, the third style came into fashion around 15 BCE. It is considerably simpler, with architectural elements such as columns or gables that are hinted at yet painted delicately, usually on a red or black background. They often look like abstract ornamentation. Egyptian motifs and ornaments are common. Mythological imagery is rarer and varies in form.

The simplicity and abstraction of the third style distinguish it clearly from the second, which was in fashion between 80 and 15 BCE. Here we have realistic architectural landscapes, sometimes with complex perspectives, composed of columns, temples and pedestals, that often look illusionistic: the wall appears to be opening. Here the second style betrays its origins in stage painting, which painted theatrical masks also recall. The representation of mythological scenes is extremely rare in the second style.

The first style is evident from the second century BCE onwards. Through painting but also stucco reliefs it imitates marble masonry. There are only occasional instances of still lifes or figurative scenes.

The painting was done on plaster that covered the walls of quarry stones and mortar. Even taverns and relatively small houses were painted; only the most modest homes and slave quarters had unpainted plaster, or none at all, leaving the bare masonry visible.

Evidently the Vettii spent a huge sum of money on having their house painted according to the latest taste. But with all their riches they didn't come close to what some long-established (or those who passed themselves off as such) families could offer. These residents deliberately left older murals in their houses, sometimes even restoring them. It's a bit like someone today living in a house with paintings or wallpaper from the eighteenth century.

The older styles can be found predominantly in the houses of the wealthy, such as the House of the Faun, the largest in Pompeii. It's almost entirely decorated in the first style, which at the time of the volcanic eruption was already 200 years old. In this way the owners were able to show that they came from a venerable family who could look back on a long history.

The Vettii were unable to do this. As nouveau-riche freedmen they were far more concerned with consigning their past as slaves to oblivion. The Greek myths and gods who decorated their house were supposed to show that they'd arrived in the upper class culturally too.

In a room with a view of the peristyle garden, where people met to drink wine and eat, the rear wall shows a naked man tied to a wheel. The educated viewer would recognise him as

Ixion, who was punished for trying to rape Juno, the wife of Jupiter. Juno is present at the punishment, sitting on a throne. The room is sometimes called the 'Ixion room' after the painting.

In the middle of the wall to the left of this picture an even more curious story is being told. We can see Daedalus, the brilliant craftsman and father of Icarus (who attempted to fly from the island of Crete with artificial wings but came too close to the sun). He's presenting Queen Pasiphaë with a cow on wheels. Her husband, King Minos of Crete, had incurred the wrath of Poseidon, the god of the sea, by sacrificing a second-rate bull to him rather than his best. As punishment Poseidon made the king's wife fall in love with the bull. The cow crafted by Daedalus was hollow inside, so Pasiphaë could hide in it and be impregnated by the bull. The result of their union would be the Minotaur, the mythical creature with a human body and a bull's head.

If you imagine the Vettii's group of friends tipsily commenting on these stories during their feasts, you realise an essential function of these pictures. They acted as inspiration for conversation, in which the guests could demonstrate their education (you had to know the myth to understand the image) as well as show off with creative or funny interpretations.

We can read about how this worked in *The Satyricon*, which has come down to us as fragments of a novel from the first century

WHAT IS IT ABOUT CLASSICAL ART?

CE, written by one Petronius (the brilliant 1969 film by Federico Fellini is highly recommended as an entry into this text).

The novel contains a long chapter, almost like a novel within a novel, which bears the title 'Trimalchio's dinner party'. Trimalchio is a freed slave who, like the Vettii, has made his fortune and who comments on the mythological pictures in his house to great comic effect. For the most part this is unintentional; he gets all the myths mixed up. In this way the text feeds the stereotype of the nouveau-riche freedman who, although he can have his house – from the walls to the crockery – enriched with Greek myths, understands little of their content. But also the game with the pictures is raised to a new level. Not only is it presumed that the guests knew and talked about the myths, the reader too must work out what Trimalchio mixes up and tells wrongly. So here we get an idea of the sophistication (and of the blunders) hiding behind the painted walls of a city like Pompeii.

The Minotaur lived trapped in a labyrinth. After losing a war the Athenians had to send seven girls and seven boys every nine years to be sacrificed to him there. Eventually the Athenian hero Theseus put an end to this gruesome ritual by killing the Minotaur. But he would never have managed it without Ariadne, King Minos's daughter, who secretly helped him. To enable him to find his way back out of the labyrinth she gave him a ball of thread that he unwound on his way in.

After this she was no longer safe with her own family, so Theseus took her on his ship. While she was sleeping he simply left her on the island of Naxos. Pretty cowardly, although in the end things turned out well for Ariadne. Nobody lesser than the god of wine, Dionysus, found her asleep and fell in love with her. The two of them became a couple, even though he was a god and she a mortal. Ariadne and Dionysus are among the most popular subjects in Pompeii. We will meet them again in the next chapter as guardians of secret rituals in the Villa of the Mysteries.

But we don't have to look far. The two of them also adorn the south wall of the Ixion room in the House of the Vettii, opposite the picture of Pasiphaë. We see them at the moment when Dionysus discovers the sleeping Ariadne. 'Discover' is meant literally here: a satyr, one of the accompanying figures to Dionysus, lifts the sleeping woman's cloak to reveal her naked body. Dionysus, standing to the left of the picture, gazes at her.

This is a good example, moreover, of a problem we're tackling in Pompeii, especially with regard to the aforementioned exhibition on 'Art and Sensuality in the Houses of Pompeii'.

Greek mythology is full of rape and sexual violence. And even if this might not be absolutely clear-cut in the case of Dionysus and Ariadne, there is undoubtedly a stark imbalance between the sleeping, passive and vulnerable woman, and the man who disrobes and desires her. An incident like this – man exposes sleeping woman – would nowadays be an obvious case for the public prosecutor. #MeToo has increased consciousness of the problem once more.

WHAT IS IT ABOUT CLASSICAL ART?

The question we're grappling with is: How can we speak about such mythological images without playing down the more or less implicit sexual violence in them, but also without falling into a modern terminology that translates the myth into our time, thus robbing it of its historical context?

Traditionally, museum texts (publications, guides, signs or apps) have often been characterised by grotesque trivialisation. This begins with the terminology. For example, we read of the 'union' between Poseidon and Medusa in the Temple of Athena (in modern parlance, Poseidon forces Medusa to have sex, for which *she* is then punished: Athena turns her into a monster) or how Ganymede is Zeus's 'favourite' (Zeus, Jupiter in Latin, abducts the boy to sexually abuse him. On top of that Ganymede has to serve as Jupiter's cup-bearer).

As these examples illustrate, it is a fundamental problem that our modern terminology has no equivalent in antiquity. Let's take the word 'rape', for instance, which I've already said abounds in Greek mythology. This act couldn't have been conveyed so directly to someone in ancient Greece because the word as such didn't exist. Our term 'rape' most closely corresponds to the ancient Greek words *biazein* and *hybrizein*, which are general terms for abuse or an atrocity in non-sexual contexts too. Similarly, the Latin word *constuprare*, where the Italian word for rape (*stupro*) comes from, means 'to dishonour, violate' but also 'to commit adultery'.

We can see that sexual violence and rape were such common features of life in antiquity that the classical languages didn't even develop a specific terminology for them. Not only does this make it difficult to describe rape in myth, we are also in danger of swinging to the other extreme. For if we now decide to construe classical-age sex in general as rape, we run the risk of retrospectively denying the female figures any vestige of agency, by blanket-defining them as victims.

This is, I believe, food for thought for the present day too. Because we ought to be asking: Are there things nowadays that future generations will say we lack the terminology for? And what could these be?

With regards to Pompeii, the difficulty is not merely translating the myth into our modern languages, but also the fact that here we're dealing with quite different groups of visitors. So not only does 'classical' need to be in the plural, but 'public' too – something that Italian can do grammatically. In the museum sector we increasingly find ourselves talking about plural *pubblici* (audiences) rather than *pubblico* (audience) in the singular.

One of the largest, but in day-to-day museum planning rather neglected, groups of visitors is children. Every year hundreds of thousands of children visit the ancient city and come face to face with sexual imagery, some of it so pornographic that it wouldn't last half an hour posted on Facebook. I speak here from experience. My first exhibition in Paestum, which was about archaeological looting, illegal art dealing and the forgery of ancient artworks, had as its lead PR image the marble torso of a naked goddess that the Italian police had seized and handed over to the museum. To promote the exhibition on social media we had to come up with another image as the algorithms on Facebook immediately identified a violation of its rules and blocked the corresponding posts. This anecdote

WHAT IS IT ABOUT CLASSICAL ART?

is not intended to be a polemic; it is rather another example of how difficult it is convey how antiquity dealt with bodies and sexuality from the perspective of today's norms.

There is no easy answer. Instead our current aim is to avoid the crassest breakdowns in communication while formulating existing texts as inclusively as possible.

What does the House of the Vettii tell us about Hermaphroditus, then? To answer this question we have to return to the Ixion room. On the rear wall we see Ixion tied to the wheel; on the wall to the left Pasiphaë and Daedalus are depicted. In the centre of the wall opposite we see Dionysus's discovery of the sleeping Ariadne on Naxos, a scene that is portrayed with great frequency in Pompeii.

But there's another picture on that wall. Above a side door Hermaphroditus is being disrobed by Pan. Pan's reaction is one of shock, as can be seen by his raised arm. The reason for this is clear from a comparison with Ariadne. Hermaphroditus is lying on the ground in a similar position to Ariadne; he was probably sleeping too. The hairstyle and body shape also resemble Ariadne's or those of one of the nymphs who appear in such numbers in Pompeian wall paintings. All of this suggests that the moment before Pan lifts the cloak of the sleeping Hermaphroditus he looks just like a young woman, be it the sleeping Ariadne or an anonymous 'nymph'.

The picture thus implies a backstory: Pan, libidinous and impulsive, approaches a young woman, thus from an ancient perspective a 'permitted' object of male desire. But when he puts his hand on her and lifts the cloak, he discovers his error: it's a male figure. According to the grammar and sexual understanding of antiquity, Hermaphroditus is a male figure. But that's not the actual problem. After all, we've already seen that homosexual relationships were accepted in certain circumstances. The problem is that Hermaphroditus's phallus is erect. He's not a passive 'catamite', no *puer delicatus*, but someone who harbours desire himself. This is made clear in the picture by the erection.

And so we have a situation not provided for by ancient sexual morality: two men with an active desire encounter each other. Phallus meets phallus. Almost everything is possible in the ancient imagination: woman with man, man with boy, even man with animal. But phallus with phallus? Never. The pictures that show the encounter between Hermaphroditus and Silenus or Pan are in fact among the few exceptions in ancient art depicting the meeting of two men with an 'active desire'.

As has been said, the assumption of women's sexual passivity in the male-dominated culture of antiquity went so far that the question of consensual sex wasn't even formulated. Correspondingly there was no specific term for rape or sexual coercion either. Whether a woman gave her consent or not seemed simply irrelevant. But what our present-day terminology would describe as a homosexual relationship was also subject to the hierarchy of active and passive. In this respect only one individual could be the male in the full sense of the word: the active, elder one, or in the Roman world the man who enjoyed full citizenship.

The images that show Hermaphroditus's encounter with an – always male – antagonist subvert this hierarchy. They open up the possibility of an imaginary erotic encounter that should never occur in reality. But if it does take place, it ends sadly.

It's not Ovid who is the literary parallel for the pictures of Hermaphroditus. As we have seen, he tells a completely different story: the feminisation of a man. The pictures, by contrast, speak of a woman who turns out to be a phallus-bearer/man.

We encounter similar tales, albeit in a quite different context, in the 'scholarly' literature of antiquity. 'It is no fable that women can change into men,' affirms Pliny the Elder, one of the leading scholarly authorities of his time (and eyewitness of the eruption of Vesuvius).[16] Certainly, if you have in your head Ovid's tale of the young man in the pool, such stories seem to have little to do with Hermaphroditus. But the moment you free yourself from the diktat of 'high literature' and allow the pictures to be pictures, it soon becomes clear that the pseudo-scholarly reports of women who are transformed into men are ultimately dealing with the same topic that we find in the pictures with Hermaphroditus at their centre – and about which Ovid says precisely nothing.

It's about the male fantasy of being surprised for a change and coming into contact with a counter-desirer instead of the 'permitted' object of lust (girl, woman, boy . . .), who is ever-passive and thus desirable, but not actively desiring. In the language of the art and culture of antiquity this counter-desirer – the desirable desirer – is symbolised by the woman with a phallus.

Diodorus Siculus, a scholarly author of the first century BCE, recounts one of the metamorphosis stories also circulated by Pliny:

> In a place called Abai in Arabia there lived a man called Diophantos of Macedonian origin. He married an Arabian woman and fathered a son named after him and a daughter called Heraïs. His son died before he reached adolescence. When the daughter appeared to be of marriageable age he wedded her to a man called Samaides. Samaides lived with his wife for a year before setting out on a long journey. But Heraïs, so it is said, was gripped by a strange and quite unbelievable illness. A severe inflammation appeared in her womb, and when the area kept swelling and she developed a serious fever, the doctors thought there must be a tumour growing on her cervix. So they tried everything they could to combat the inflammation. On the seventh day, however, her skin tore and from Heraïs's genitals a male penis and testicles appeared. When this breach occurred by chance there was no doctor or other outsider present, just the mother and two maids. They were speechless with astonishment at the bizarre incident, gave Heraïs the appropriate care and kept silent about what had happened.[17]

WHAT IS IT ABOUT CLASSICAL ART?

When Heraïs's husband returns from his journey she feels ashamed and refuses sexual intercourse. Her husband takes her to court to claim his 'marital right'. Heraïs says nothing and keeps her women's clothes on the whole time. But when the jury is about to find against her, she removes her robe to show everyone her male genitalia. This allows her to win the case. After the divorce from her husband Samaides, who will later take his own life, she changes her name and lives as a man.

That's Diodorus's report. What is revealing is the question Heraïs asks the jury once she's revealed her sex: Should a man be forced to have sex with a man? Here we can see that body image and eroticism in antiquity obeyed rules that in some ways are certainly not the same as ours today, but were no less binding. Things were done differently, no doubt, but there was also less freedom than classical archaeology pioneer Winckelmann, among wigs and corsets, may have dreamed of. An unfamiliar world, but not one that was necessarily better.

But the fact that this unfamiliar world keeps prompting us to challenge established hierarchies and supposedly natural circumstances makes it in my view worthwhile to keep engaging with classical art today – in spite of everything. Or precisely because of everything that is contradictory and unsettling in this art.

CHAPTER TWO
CAPTIVATING RITUALS

Anybody who talks today about classical art must anticipate a cynical reaction from those who've decided that 'art' and 'artists' in the modern sense didn't exist before the Renaissance. European art historians in particular like to champion this view, which of course might be true on a purely superficial level (and at the same time emphasises the supposedly universal uniqueness of European modernity, but that's another problem). But this is the point: it's only on a purely superficial level. In the 'modern sense' the figure of the artist, and everything we associate with this (genius, madness, originality, role of the social outsider), of course only exists in modernity. The fact, however, that a similar understanding of art existed in antiquity is proven not least by Roman art historiography. As discussed in the previous chapter, the Romans saw the art of ancient Greece as a classical ideal for their own art and culture. And thus arose an academic interest in the development of Greek art.

The notion that a completely new conception of art emerged with the Renaissance does contain a kernel of truth, though ultimately it doesn't withstand close scrutiny. According to this idea, the art of the modern age, that's to say the period since the Middle Ages, is characterised by the radical liberation of the artist from religious and social constraints. In truth, the mantra of the freedom of art is something that would have been hard to get across to people in the Middle Ages or antiquity. In this respect the Renaissance, and the modern age it ushered in, really does represent a watershed.

But the rhetoric of liberation contains a value judgement. One could put it more neutrally and say that in the modern age art and religion increasingly decoupled, ultimately becoming two separate systems. From a global historical perspective that is indeed exceptional, albeit not unique. After all, we've already seen in the case of Apollo the Citharist from Pompeii that religious concerns no longer played a role in this representation of the divinity that was only superficially pious.

In history it is generally the case that art and religion are closely interlinked. It seems doubtful that in the early millennia of human history there was any art that *wasn't* religious. For wherever we look, creativity and artistic drive are first seen in religious objects, be they in collective ritual places or private sanctuaries. This isn't just true of the visual arts, but of writing, music and dance too.

Classical antiquity is no exception here. Indeed, thanks to the written records that have survived we can reconstruct how this archaic understanding of art continued to be influential long into the historic era and eventually into the Christian art of the Middle Ages.

CAPTIVATING RITUALS

It took a long time, however, for modern research to become aware of the religious nature of antique art. There are few places where this is so clear as the British Museum, the monument to imperial collecting zeal, driven by the ambition to exhibit the art of the entire world in the capital of the empire. Among the controversial acquisitions are the so-called Elgin Marbles, classical sculptures which the British ambassador to the Ottoman Empire, Lord Elgin, took from the Acropolis in Athens at the beginning of the nineteenth century and sold to the British Museum. The basis for this was the permission granted by the Ottoman authorities to 'take a few stones away'. Elgin interpreted the consent generously; among the 'stones' he had removed was almost the entire frieze of the Parthenon, the largest temple of the Acropolis, built in the fifth century BCE under the supervision of the famous sculptor Phidias.[18]

The debate about the return of the Elgin Marbles, conducted on the Greek side with great passion, was given fresh impetus in 2009 with the inauguration of the new Acropolis Museum in Athens. Space was deliberately left for the marble artworks in London, including the Parthenon Frieze. As well as admiring countless ancient exhibits, visitors to the museum also see a host of empty spaces, which declare better than any political statement that something is missing here.

Apart from the issue of *where* the frieze ought to be displayed in future (London or Athens) there is also the question of *how* to present such a work to the public. The display in London was mounted after the purchase sanctioned by Parliament in 1816 and it reflects the understanding of ancient art at the time. The frieze is installed along the walls of the room at eye level. Just as in an art gallery, everything is designed to allow the viewer to fully enjoy the artwork in all its detail.

The problem is that this doesn't correspond at all to how the frieze was displayed in antiquity. It used to crown the exterior walls of the cella, the central sanctuary of the temple, surrounded by columns. It was thus 13 metres above ground level, in the shadow of the columned halls around the temple. To get a vague idea of the 160-metre-long frieze you had to strain your neck somewhat. It was practically impossible to make out the many details, originally rendered in colour.

The gable sculptures are similarly baffling. In the British Museum you can walk around them and thereby admire the perfect craftsmanship at the rear of the sculptures too. But in antiquity the pieces adorned the pediments of the temple, 17 metres above the ground. It would have been impossible to see the backs of these sculptures.

Why did the Athenians invest so much time and money in artworks that they could only 'enjoy' to a limited extent? Why did they commission the most famous artists of the time to create sculptures that were displayed in a way that nobody could appreciate them in all their detail? Why did they spend the money of the Delian League, which was for defence purposes, on a temple and its decoration? (By way of comparison, imagine NATO funding a museum of contemporary art out of its military budget.)

The answer lies in the religious nature of ancient art. The temple and all its accessories were dedicated to the goddess Athena; they belonged to her, not only in a religious sense but legally too. She mustn't be offered anything less than perfect.

CAPTIVATING RITUALS

The frieze and the other sculptures were, therefore, not art in the modern sense, geared towards consumption, but part of a dialogue between humans and gods conducted by votive offerings, rites and prayer. Essentially these were 'magical' images; it was believed they had an effect beyond their purely aesthetic function. If no earthly viewer was able to see every feature of the frieze in all its detail, not a single feature escaped the goddess Athena's attention.

Whereas in London the Parthenon Frieze was displayed in art-gallery style, in Pompeii the practice was still to prise out the wall paintings from the plaster and take them to the royal museum in Portici, later in Naples. Pompeii represented less an open-air museum than a sort of mine where ancient artworks were 'quarried' for the royal collections. The process was a selective one. In the main it was mythological scenes that were detached and taken away, whereas the wall decorations framing them remained in situ. Sadly, these often fell victim to the wind and weather, and today are only known from old engravings and descriptions.

It is undeniable that there were also conservation reasons for the removal of the murals in the eighteenth and early nineteenth centuries. At the time there was no way of conserving the frescoes in situ. Even now the preservation of wall paintings is one of the greatest challenges in Pompeii. Together with the restorers at the park we are continually striving to swap ideas about methods and approaches that might help us achieve this.

The voices arguing for preservation in situ became ever louder over the years. Nowadays frescoes and statues are removed from the site only in exceptional circumstances. The goal is – as can be seen at the thermopolium (a kind of ancient street-food restaurant) that was excavated in 2020 and first made accessible to the public in 2021 – to reproduce the status of 79 CE exactly, including the cooking pots and amphorae that stood on the counter or leaned against it.

Remarkably, an Italian scholar by the name of Scipione Maffei, in view of the excavations in nearby Herculaneum using underground tunnels, already formulated this approach in 1748, the year Pompeii was discovered. What an extraordinary adventure it would be, according to Maffei, 'to uncover a whole city rather than just one or other monument'.[19]

Goethe, too, who visited the site on his Italian journey, was less impressed by the artworks salvaged from Pompeii than by the ancient city as a sort of total artwork. In his journal entry for 13 March 1787 he notes: 'The houses are small and cramped but inside all painted most delicately. The city gate is strange, with the graves right next to it. The grave of a priestess, made like a semicircular bench with a stone backrest, the inscription carved in big letters. Above the backrest you can see the sea and the setting sun. A wonderful place, worthy of the beautiful thought.'[20]

A few days later, on 18 March, when Goethe visited the museum in Portici where the discoveries from Pompeii could be marvelled at (although visitors were strictly forbidden from making sketches or notes), he mentally transposed what he'd seen into that 'disappeared time, where all these things stood around their owners to be actively used and enjoyed'.

But he hadn't forgotten how 'small and cramped' the houses were that caught his attention when visiting the excavations: 'Those small houses and rooms in Pompeii now seem both more cramped and more spacious; more cramped because I imagined them stuffed with many valuable objects, more spacious because these very objects were not just temporary but artistically decorated in the most ingenious and dainty fashion, a delight for the senses and broadening the mind more than the roomiest house could ever do.'

Without doubt Goethe's reaction is heavily influenced by the aesthetic sensibilities of his era. But his mention of the usage of the objects points to another context. Here Goethe is referring to the experience of the ancient world where the meaning of the objects, whether artworks or not, developed through the accomplishment of everyday tasks.

Within this context of ancient experience, ritual played a considerably bigger role than in our modern understanding of art, at least in the early period of ancient cultures. Originally, statues and paintings were first and foremost votive offerings to the gods. As we have seen, over the course of antiquity such objects were increasingly regarded as artworks in the modern sense, for which there was a corresponding market as well as specialist literature. But from a historical point of view – and here modern art history is right to emphasise the break with antiquity – Apollo the Citharist is far more closely related to a primitive clay vessel offered to the gods in the early era of

Pompeii than to a Neoclassical sculpture by, say, Antonio Canova. Although outwardly the two may look similar, they were created and viewed in completely different worlds. Even during the centuries of gradual emancipation of artistic creation from the sphere of religion, the original religious function of art remained present. And this can be seen in Pompeii too.

We can't know what Goethe would have said about what is probably the best-known fresco cycle in Pompeii, because the frieze, which takes its name from the Villa of the Mysteries on the road to Herculaneum, wasn't discovered until 1909. According to the current interpretation, it shows a mystery rite, although we should not interpret 'mystery' here in its modern sense. In Greek the *mystes* is the person inducted into a cult that is 'closed' to outsiders (from *myein*, to close something such as one's eyes or mouth), and who has become acquainted with its secret (*mysterium*).

This highlights the main problem facing research into antique mystery cults: because the rites and prayers had to be kept secret, even contemporaries in antiquity were puzzled by what was actually going on. Today, after two millennia, it is virtually impossible to obtain any clarity on the matter. It's not made any simpler by the fact that some of the little that we have from the ancient sources only goes back to Christian authors of late antiquity. These had no first-hand knowledge, of course, and they were not unbiased. Their main concern was to disparage and ridicule the 'heathen' faith.

And yet from the perspective of antiquity, Christianity was itself a mystery cult. Echoes of this can still be found today, when for example in the Catholic liturgy priests speak of the transubstantiation of bread and wine: 'the mystery of faith', in Latin *mysterium fidei*.

The common feature of ancient mystery cults was the induction or initiation, which in Christianity occurs through baptism. Joining a mystery cult and being initiated into its secrets assumes an act of will. You acknowledge – or in Christian terms 'convert to' – the rules and dogmas of the cult community. When Christianity later moved over to baptising newborns, the idea of an act of will was turned on its head. Hence the efforts to make up for this later in life through first communion, confirmation, rebaptism etc.

Connected to the initiation is a promise of salvation: those who stick to the rules and commandments and follow the prescribed rites can hope for redemption. In ancient mystery cults the promise of salvation is also related to life after death, but not exclusively. Rather, initiation heralds a 'new life', which foresees redemption and salvation prior to death, at least in part. Trance and mystic union – the *unio mystica* of Christian theology experienced in communion – anticipate in the here and now the transcendental salvation of the mortal creature.

The notion of the 'new life' explains why there is something of a symbolic death in every initiation. The inductee 'dies', leaving behind their previous life, to be 'reborn' as an initiate. The ancient Greek writer Plutarch (first to second century CE) compared the so-called Greater Mysteries in Eleusis, not far from Athens, which were celebrated in honour of the fertility goddess Demeter, to a near-death experience that he evidently knew through authentic reports. And in his novel *The Golden Ass*, Apuleius of Madaura (second century CE) writes of the mysteries of the Egyptian goddess Isis (who also had a temple and flourishing cult community in Pompeii) that the initiation was celebrated as a 'voluntary death and a salvation granted on request' by the goddess.[21]

The idea of the 'new life' is also very present in the Christian doctrine of salvation, and it wasn't something merely added to the faith later. Jesus emphasises this fact at several points in the New Testament including in what I consider to be one of the most impressive verses of the Bible, which appears twice (Matthew 16:25 and Luke 9:24): 'For whoever will save his life shall lose it: and whoever will lose his life for my sake shall find it.'

When these words were spoken and communicated more widely, eventually to be adopted into the New Testament canon, life was still pulsating in Pompeii. We will return later to the sparse evidence of early Christians in and around Pompeii. The fact is, in this city another 'new god' trumped all the others in popularity: Dionysus, known in Italy as Liber or Bacchus.

That he should be 'new' seems odd at first, given that his name appears on Bronze Age clay tablets from the second millennium BCE in Greece. According to these, Dionysus was an ancient Mediterranean god of fertility and vegetation. But this describes only one aspect of his nature. The other is that, despite being so long established, he remains a stranger. Dionysus is the eternal outsider. He's not a member of the official club of the twelve Olympian gods. In Homer and Hesiod, the poets who 'gave the Greeks their gods', he plays no role worth mentioning. He doesn't have a fixed place outside Olympus either, which is reflected in the mythology by the fact that he is permanently itinerant, a nomad among the gods. With his retinue of satyrs and maenads, intoxicated by wine, drumming and flute music, he moves through lands, even getting as far as India to proclaim his tidings of joy. He wants to be accepted by people, another thing that marks him out from the Olympian gods.

Nobody had to 'believe' in Apollo, Athena or Zeus. They existed; there was as little doubt about this as about the existence of air or water. With Dionysus it was different. He had to win over his supporters, often having to overcome resistance. He was a 'new' god because he always had to be accepted anew. That's why he's called *theos neos*, 'new god', in Euripides's tragedy *The Bacchae*, first performed in 405 BCE in Athens.

The play tells the story of the King of Thebes, Pentheus, who rejects the cult of Dionysus along with his night-time orgies. Dionysus then appears before the king in the form of a stranger and confronts him. Pentheus digs in his heels, even prepared to take up arms against the god's followers, but in the end his hostility costs him his life. Persuaded by Dionysus, he sneaks into the mountains dressed as a woman to watch what the 'Bacchae', the women of the city who have fallen into a Dionysian trance, get up to. The women, including Pentheus's mother Agave, spot him sitting in a tree and in their madness tear him to pieces. This scene is depicted in the 'Pentheus room' of the House of the Vettii, which we looked at in the previous chapter.

The Bacchae was one of the most popular tragedies in antiquity and is still performed today. The play was known far beyond the borders of Greece – definitely in Roman Italy, as the House of the Vettii shows, but also in Parthia and Armenia, as proven by a story passed down about the death of the Roman general Crassus.

Crassus was the rich but dull third member of the triumvirate with Caesar and Pompey. He strove to achieve military victories on a par with those of his colleagues. By way of comparison, Caesar was about to subjugate the whole of Gaul, an area roughly corresponding to modern-day France and Belgium. To better this, Crassus attacked the most powerful opponent he could find at the time: the Parthian Empire, whose centre lay in modern-day Iran. But the enterprise went badly. In 53 BCE Crassus's legions were defeated at Carrhae and he was killed soon afterwards – there is some debate about exactly how. His severed head was brought to the Parthian king Orodes II in Artashat, the capital of the Armenian Empire that was allied to him. The messenger arrived with his macabre trophy just as the king was attending a performance at the theatre. So the story goes, an actor spontaneously picked up Crassus's head, which had been thrown into the middle of the room, and recited the following verse:

CAPTIVATING RITUALS

> From the mountains we bring
> A freshly cut tendril to the palace.
> A wonderful prey.²²

These are the words in Euripides's *The Bacchae* with which Pentheus's mother Agave presents the head of her son, whom in her madness she's failed to recognise, to the royal palace at Thebes.

Around the same time that King Orodes is supposed to have heard Euripides's verses in Artashat, the frieze in the Villa of the Mysteries was created, at the centre of which are enthroned Dionysus and Ariadne. The frieze belongs to the second style of Pompeian wall paintings and thus dates from the period between 80 and 15 BCE. Details suggest that it was painted between 50 and 30 BCE.

The popularity of *The Bacchae* and the mystery frieze both reflect the key role that Dionysus played in the ancient world, despite or probably because of his outsider status. For anyone who joined his following could hope for redemption from earthly cares and worries. Lysios, the deliverer, he was also called. As this promise tended to appeal to everyone, irrespective of nationality or sex – even to the slaves who in antiquity were considered 'subhuman' – enthusiasm for the Dionysus cult cut through all social strata.

The cult of Dionysus, which had endless local manifestations, thus functioned as a sort of melting pot for all manner of mystical currents and initiation rites that had proliferated since the fourth century BCE. One of the most prominent was ascribed to the mythical singer Orpheus, who more or less appears as a prophet of Dionysus. The connection between Orpheus and Dionysus isn't revealed in mythology, as would usually be the case (the two are neither related nor do their paths cross), but instead in the ritual practice that developed through creative reinterpretations over time.

In the House of Orpheus in Pompeii, situated on Via del Vesuvio and excavated in 1874, Orpheus is depicted making music, surrounded by wild animals listening spellbound. Through his music the divine singer was able to overcome all linguistic boundaries and even those between species. The life-size painting was placed in the garden, which thus became part of the imagery, and was visible through the entrance to those passing by.

Outside the gates of Pompeii was an old temple to Dionysus, its gable relief showing him together with Ariadne. The gable sculptures are now exhibited in the Antiquarium, the park's museum. But more than in the public temple his cult probably flourished in the countless private cult communities and associations that must have existed in Pompeii, of which both the mystery frieze and the mural in the House of Orpheus seem to be evidence.

But what explains the fascination that Dionysus clearly exerted on people throughout the entire Roman world and beyond? To understand this we must look at what the traditional religions of the ancient world had to offer.

No conversion, no sworn-in cult community, no redemption. Compared to the initiation cults such as that of Dionysus, but also to Christianity, the spiritual offering of the traditional religions of Greece and Rome boils down to this formula. With the established gods promises of salvation were in short supply, which must have been a major reason for the success of the 'new god', be it Dionysus or the Christian god. People in search of what today would be called personal faith or a spiritual path just couldn't find anything like that among the traditional Mediterranean religions.

The cults of ancient Italy go back to the prehistoric period. At the time, as we can infer from surviving remnants of archaic rites, there was no distinction between the world and the gods, the profane and the sacred. Religious behaviour was so firmly anchored in daily life that there could be no thought of religion as something 'otherworldly'. Deities were present in everything: springs, rivers, mountains, trees. But the house, field and stable too, even war and politics, were subject to their own gods, guardian spirits and natural spirits. Particular importance was accorded to ancestors, who were honoured at their graves and occupied an intermediary role between people and gods.

We find relics of these archaic forms of religion in the writings passed down to us. In his book *The Golden Bough*, which first appeared in 1890, James George Frazer assessed the sources for this. His work contains some dubious generalisations and speculation, but its enduring popularity beyond academia proves that Frazer hit a nerve. Anyone who reads the book (and/or – as I highly recommend – watches the beginning of Pasolini's feature film *Medea*, which was strongly influenced by it) will discover that ancient religion has very unclassical roots, which is basically correct. This religion is more reminiscent of the rituals and customs of so-called 'primitive' indigenous peoples rather than of the ideal picture of white marble antiquity. What the texts of the classical era transmit to us is already a development of these archaic roots of religiosity, which were subsequently adapted for life in ever-growing cities.

From the numerous examples revealing that traditional religion meant little to most people in the classical era, we can cite here a particularly striking one, the Roman *flamines* (singular: *flamen*). These were the priests of the most important deities of the Roman state, a total of fifteen in number: three *flamines maiores* ('high priests') and twelve *flamines minores* ('lesser priests'). But if we look at the names of the gods they served, we see that barely any of them are known to history. The highest priests of the Roman state served gods, about most of whom we know little more than the name. And in the case of two of the *flamines minores*, we don't even have any clues about which gods they were allocated to. The three high *flamines* served Jupiter, Mars and Quirinus – so far so good. But things get tricky with the lesser *flamines*. They were responsible for the cults of Carmenta, Ceres, Falacer, Flora, Furrina, Palatua, Pomona, Portunus, Vulcan and Volturnus. Those who don't know these names shouldn't worry; apart from Ceres, the goddess of the fields and cereals (comparable to the Greek Demeter), and Vulcan, the god of fire and metalworking (whose Greek counterpart is Hephaestus), they are unfamiliar even to seasoned scholars of antiquity.

CAPTIVATING RITUALS

In most cases the character of the deities can be guessed at from the names. Flora ('flower, blossom'), for example, was probably associated with the season of spring. Portunus (related to *porta*, 'door', and *portus*, 'harbour') was the god of gates and boundaries, but also of harbours and livestock, one of the most important trading goods in early times. Pomona comes from *pomum*, 'apple, fruit' (the word lives on in the French for apple and potato: *pomme* and *pomme de terre*).

These are gods who were associated with nature, agriculture and village life. In Rome, traces of this archaic religion were preserved because the village became the capital of the Mediterranean world. We must imagine the archaic cults at Vesuvius prior to the foundation of Pompeii around 600 BCE to have been similar, although here far fewer written sources have survived.

The two oldest shrines in the city – that of Apollo in the forum and Athena/Minerva near the theatre district – show the influence of the Etruscans, a people from central Italy who settled in various places in Campania at the time (such as Capua and Pontecagnano) and were also significantly involved in the founding of Pompeii. The early inscriptions of Pompeii, which are dedications to the gods, are without exception written in the Etruscan language. Excavations in a sanctuary outside the city walls called Fondo Iozzino, carried out under the direction of my predecessor Massimo Osanna, have emphatically confirmed this: since 2014, when the new excavations began, more than seventy Etruscan inscriptions have been added to the fifteen already known from the Apollo shrine. Pompeii is thus the place with the most Etruscan inscriptions outside Etruria, an area that encompassed most of modern-day Tuscany, northern Lazio and north-west Umbria.

The temples and cults of the new city that superseded the hamlets and villages at the foot of Vesuvius are thus part of a far-reaching, radical change. Etruscans and Greeks set the agenda, and the momentum of the times was towards modernisation and urbanisation. This includes the use of writing, which is identifiable for the first time here in Pompeii, as well as the building of new temples. Their colourful clay roofs were created by Etruscan and Greek artists, itinerant forerunners of the new era. It is the city that gives rise to completely new forms of politics, administration, business, culture and religion. The primitive and archaic nature of religion was less manifest in the newfangled buildings and statues, but lived on even more strongly in the rituals.

This becomes evident in the aforementioned sanctuary of Fondo Iozzino outside the walls of Pompeii. The sanctuary lay on a small hill, surrounded by reeds near the mouth of the River Sarno (Latin Sarnus), which connected the coast to the mountainous interior. The river in its entirety was regarded as something sacred, embodied by the river god of the same name who is depicted as a bearded giant on a painted house altar in Pompeii (in the House of the Sarno Lararium).

The sanctuary of Fondo Iozzino consisted of a walled precinct. No temple was ever built there. The classical notion that no sanctuary must be without a temple as a 'house of the god' was a relatively late development; in the archaic imagination the deities 'lived' in mountains, rivers, springs, in the sky, on the seabed or beneath the earth. Following the recent excavations, it is believed that the latter was the case in the sanctuary of Fondo Iozzino. This is indicated by the many vessels that were left upside down on the ground. Chemical analyses have shown that these contained wine, which must have been poured into the earth here as a ritual; the vessels remained afterwards as a kind of reminder.

Such rites suggest a belief in gods and goddesses that lived in the earth, thereby having a special connection to the realm of the dead, but also representing the fertility of the soil. Offering the deities a share of the harvest, especially of such a valuable and prestigious product as wine, was a sort of necessary exchange for early peasant societies: you give back to the gods and nature spirits a share of what they allow you to grow, so you can count on their continued benevolence in the future. Besides libations and the vessels used for this purpose, other gifts to the gods were found in the sanctuary of Fondo Iozzino: weapons, Greek oil containers, jewellery and – much later, at a time when Greek art and culture were already booming in Pompeii – a series of beautiful clay statues that were probably offered to the goddess worshipped here (perhaps Ceres) beside a male deity, and which today can be seen in the Antiquarium at Pompeii.

This example clearly demonstrates the original context of ancient art. In terms of their function, the statues are direct successors to the plain clay vessels from the late seventh and sixth centuries BCE that were gifted to the gods.

I only realised the full significance of this observation after finishing my studies in Berlin, when I went to Italy and began working with Massimo Osanna. At the time neither of us could have dreamed that one day I would succeed him as director of the world-famous archaeological park.

At the beginning of 2007 I was an academic assistant at the German Archaeological Institute in Rome. On a practical level this meant working on a project to measure the archaeological remains of Gabii, an old city in the vicinity of Rome, of which today there are only scattered ruins. I was also looking for a subject for my PhD. At a conference organised by the institute, where I had to carry the microphone around and pour coffee in the breaks, I met Osanna, who at the time was working at the University of Basilicata in Matera in southern Italy and, together with a colleague from Rome, had embarked on his own research project in Gabii.

In one of the breaks, I plucked up the courage to speak to him, asking if there might be an opportunity for me to work on the new project. Surprisingly, he listened patiently to what I said over the course of a few minutes in my imperfect Italian. At the end he told me to send him my master's dissertation and CV.

There was another test to pass. I was given permission to excavate in Gabii on a month's trial with Italian doctoral and undergraduate students. This was to be considered a privilege; to do it I had to take unpaid leave from the German Archaeological Institute. But it was worth it, as although I'd already done some excavating in Italy, I'd never worked in a purely Italian team before. It wasn't just enlightening professionally, I also found the

Bronze statue of Apollo the Citharist from the house of the same name in Pompeii.
The statue is kept in the National Archaeological Museum in Naples.

Cast of a boy who died in the 'Garden of the Fugitives' on the southern fringes of Pompeii when Mount Vesuvius erupted.

Sculpture of a young fisherman asleep that once decorated a fountain in the House of M. Epidius Rufus.

Towering above the city is Mount Vesuvius; to the left is the rear wall of the Stabian baths.

Plaster casts of victims of the eruption in the 'Garden of the Fugitives'.

View of the city from the Tower of Mercury.

A crossroads in Pompeii with one of the public fountains that was connected to an aqueduct.

Reproduction of the bronze statue of the goddess Diana, which was displayed alongside that of her brother in the Apollo sanctuary.

The painting of Leda and the swan, discovered in 2018 gave this house its name: House of Leda.

Bronze lampstand in the form of a naked boy, from the
House of Marcus Fabius Rufus.

Wall decoration in the first style in the House of the Four Styles.

Mural in the second style in the Villa of the Mysteries.

Mural in the third style in the House of the Orchard.

Mural in the fourth style in the House of the Dioscuri.

Depiction of Venus in the House of the Prince of Naples.

The peristyle in the House of the Vettii.

The Ixion room in the House of the Vettii, painted in the fourth style.

North wall: Daedalus shows Pasiphaë the hollow cow she's going to hide in.

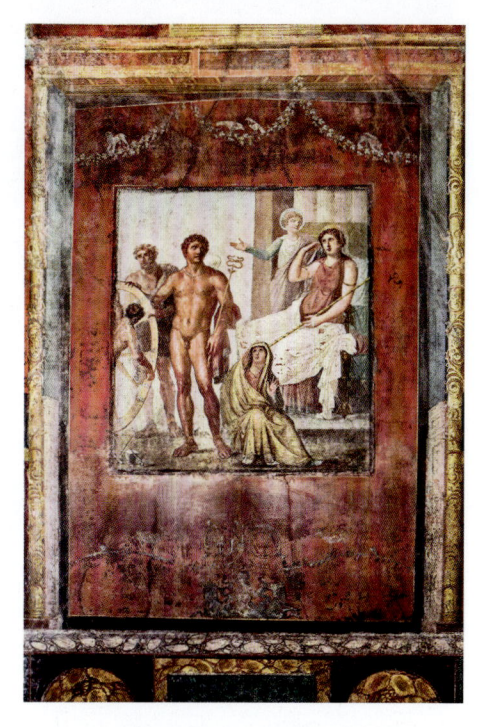

East wall: Ixion is tied to the wheel. Juno watches from her throne.

South wall: Dionysus discovers the sleeping Ariadne.

On the southern wall above the door: the encounter between Pan and Hermaphroditus.

The room with the frieze of Cupids in the House of the Vettii.

Detail from the frieze of Cupids. The Cupids are selling wine,
just like the real owners of the house.

The Pentheus room in the House of the Vettii, painted in the fourth style. The central picture shows Pentheus being torn to pieces by his mother and the other Bacchae.

A thermopolium excavated in Pompeii in 2020. Warm food and wine were sold from these kitchens, but there was nowhere to sit. People either ate on the street or took the food home.

interpersonal atmosphere far more relaxing and less competitive than in the German excavations I'd been part of.

Whether this subjective assessment could withstand an objective, statistical analysis, I cannot say. At any rate, the experience strengthened my sense that I somehow fitted in better in Italy. Indeed, friends who know me both as a 'German' and an 'Italian' tell me that the Italian version of me is considerably more extrovert, even though I didn't learn the language till I was an adult. But I've noticed that in German I tend to mull over the right expression, whereas in Italian I simply chatter away. With Italian sentence construction (verb at the beginning, not at the end as in German, adjective after the noun) you can improvise astonishingly long sentences, which almost makes you feel as if the language is speaking itself.

When I got Italian citizenship in 2020 practical concerns were in fact irrelevant for me. The legal debate about *direttori stranieri*, foreign directors like myself who had been allowed to participate in the selection process for the first time in 2014, had already been decided by the highest Italian administrative court in favour of opening up museum jobs to international competition. As melodramatic as it may sound, it was more of a matter of the heart when I swore my oath of allegiance to the Italian constitution in the presence of the mayor of Matera. I felt that dual citizenship was appropriate to the life I was living.

Thirteen years earlier I was delighted when Osanna, clearly satisfied with my work, helped me gain access to the finds from the so-called eastern sanctuary of Gabii, which had been lifted from the earth during an excavation in the 1970s and slumbering ever since in storage. I was keen to investigate the early period of the small sanctuary outside the walls of the ancient city, to find out something about how archaic rites of prehistoric Italy adjusted to the changing social, cultural and political conditions. What became of peasant farming and nature cults when scattered hamlets became a city – a city that, from our perspective, might be more comparable to a village, but nonetheless as a new form of human settlement marked a radical change back then.

In the sanctuary was a small temple, a rectangular building, its painted roof tiles the only ornamentation. But this wasn't built until the end of the sixth century BCE, that is to say the end of the timespan I was dealing with. Apart from the sparse ruins of the foundations of an older temple, all that remained from the preceding centuries, during which Gabii developed from scattered peasant huts into a city, were shards of clay vessels used for rituals inside the sanctuary then left as 'ritual rubbish'. What became 'sacred' through its use during a rite was not allowed to leave the locality of the deity. This also explains the finds in the sanctuary of Fondo Iozzino outside the walls of Pompeii, which have allowed us to understand the centuries-long history of the cult site.

After twelve months' work in the depot of the antiquities department in Gabii my database comprised 23,800 objects, 95 per cent of which were clay shards. I'd made over 600 drawings and documented countless comparable pieces in museums and libraries of the surrounding area. My wife still teases me about the time after work I rode my Vespa back from Rome to Gabii just to check the profile of a single shard for which I'd found a new comparison. When our daughter was born in 2008 we'd just returned to Berlin. She would go to sleep in our small Kreuzberg flat to the sound of the mouse clicks as I turned the 600 pencil drawings into vector graphics.

Getting excited by a nondescript shard of pottery or worked up by an academic colleague's imprecise dating – these are probably things that make archaeologists appear like oddballs to everyone else. Why such passion? Once again the answer has got to do with the engine that drives us. And which often – through our own fault – remains hidden to the outside world.

Strictly speaking I was never a 'pupil' of Massimo Osanna. I didn't study under him, nor was he my supervisor. Nonetheless for me he was what the Italians call a *maestro*. Because through my work with him – in seminars, excavations, publications and conservation – I learned a great deal. Most importantly, he taught me that archaeology is something that ultimately must benefit the wider public. We mustn't sit on the knowledge we accumulate; people who make our work possible in the first place through entrance tickets or tax revenue need to have a share in it. Second, I learned that archaeology is teamwork – more so now than ever – which isn't possible without respect for other disciplines, even those outside Classics: restoration, architecture, geology, chemistry, botany etc.

But through Osanna I also became acquainted with the approach that was the engine that got me through the 23,800 shards of pottery from Gabii: archaeology as religious studies, which I'd only touched on tangentially during my studies in Germany. In Italy this branch of archaeology is much further developed.

In truth it's impossible to understand ancient art and culture if you don't understand them as part of a world in which literally every aspect of life was structured by religious ritual. The rite is like a language in itself that structured all areas of society, its grammar and vocabulary inextricably linked to what was communicated in this society. For us today not only is the 'language' of the ancient rite difficult to decipher; as children of an age in which rituals barely feature, we also almost completely lack the corresponding grammar. Understanding ancient rituals is thus a bit like trying to learn to swim in the middle of a desert.

Nowhere is this better understood than in religious studies, a discipline whose representatives view the enthusiasm of Italian archaeology for ancient ritual with a degree of suspicion. Can anything emerge from the translation of the complicated 'language' of ritual if you leave it to archaeologists who specialise in material legacies?

The debate about this soon becomes heated, especially if it's not conducted in the cool atmosphere of the lecture theatre but over a glass of Corsican wine. Paris on a rainy day in early April 2022: in the morning I give a lecture on Doric temples at the École Pratique des Hautes Études, where all criticism and dissent is packaged politely and academically. In the evening, at a Corsican restaurant in the fifth arrondissement, we get down to the nitty-gritty. Present are Gabriella Pironti, a Neapolitan by birth and professor of ancient Greek religious history in Paris, and Claude Pouzadoux, an archaeologist who for ten years ran a French research centre in Naples before she rather ruefully returned to the cold north. We speak in Italian, first about this and that, then about mystery cults as depicted in the frieze of the Villa of the Mysteries in Pompeii, according to current interpretation.

Certain attacks are only admissible among friends because they can be seen as a vote of confidence. After some initial skirmishes (Does it make sense to talk about mystery *religions*? Everyone agrees no: at best we could speak of mystery *cults*), Gabriella lands a surprise blow. The problem is, she says, that most archaeologists don't properly understand ancient polytheism, unconsciously conceiving it in juxtaposition to monotheism. Unimpressed by the complexity that characterises even seemingly simple figures such as Hera and Zeus, they fall on mystery cults that they try to prove are everywhere, from the Tomb of the Diver in Paestum to the Villa of the Mysteries in Pompeii. It's all the fault of the Christian tradition, Gabriella argues. Indeed, it is probably no coincidence if the search for the spiritual dimensions of ancient religion has resulted in such important outcomes as on the Italian peninsula, the original home of Catholicism. Although (or maybe because?) I am an Italian by choice I feel this is aimed at me; after all, Italy has become my home not least because of the archaeology of ancient rituals. These moments of uncertainty are what constitute true research. Moments in which you suddenly sense the 'beam that is in thine own eye' behind familiar views; in other words, the subjective, biographical lens through which we perceive antiquity. And so the politely aloof questions and comments of the morning in the lecture hall are less important than the confrontation with your own history in the evening at the Corsican restaurant, when personal memory (as a child in church, the lurid-red wounds on the crucifix, incense in the air, the Swabian singsong of the intercessory prayers . . .) overlaps with academic investigation (Why the Villa of the Mysteries? Isn't there anything more important in Pompeii?).

Such moments bring us in contact with antiquity because the excavation finds suddenly interact with our own worldview; moments that this book would like to encourage, because in my education I too would have wished for more encouragement in this respect.

In the course of my teaching at the University of Naples, I sometimes try to get the students to do this, with mixed results. Those who take archaeology courses don't normally expect to be confronted with personal matters, and of course nobody ought to be forced to. I just don't think that one can continue down the academic path without addressing the issue of what drives us on. It's better to deal with it openly, as the most damaging complexes are those that are suppressed.

Ideally, we would approach a particular area of interest with an awareness of our internal engine. This awareness is also an enormous help in changing opinions when new insights emerge, for once you've acknowledged your inner motivations, you can let go of them if they prove unproductive.

A thought experiment can clearly illustrate that a reflective relationship to the past, that's to say one that recognises your own biographical and cultural influences, is the only sensible approach of any historical or art-historical research. A misunderstanding of Gabriella Pironi's argument during our discussion over dinner might lead you to assume that it would be better not to be a Catholic, nor harbour any potential conflict of interest with respect to objective research into antiquity. But taken to its logical conclusion, this would mean us having to work with the things to which we have the least emotional connection. Taken to extremes in our interconnected world, this would mean a different planet altogether. And one with which we have had no previous contact, because as soon as we encounter this planet, new 'conflicts of interest' form. The idea is absurd, of course. As individuals and as a society, we cannot help but follow our interests when investigating the past. Objectivity can only develop from critical discussion with others, and it remains a goal that research in the humanities can never quite attain.

———

The Villa of the Mysteries is a particularly eloquent example here, because the meaning of the frieze to which the complex owes its name remains disputed today. Its excavation was the work of one of Pompeii's greatest directors, Amedeo Maiuri. In 1924, at the age of thirty-eight, he became *soprintendente alle antichità* ('head of antiquities') for the whole of southern Italy, including Pompeii and the National Archaeological Museum in Naples, where many finds from Pompeii were kept. He held this post until 1961, dying two years later. He steered Pompeii through its darkest hour in the more than 250-year-history of excavations (and hopefully for a very long time to come too). On 24 August 1943 the Allied air forces began bombing Pompeii and the surrounding area with the goal of destroying the German positions along the coast, in preparation for the landing of Allied troops on the Gulf of Salerno, south of Pompeii.

On the morning after the first night of bombing Maiuri sent the following 'phonogram' by telephone to the ministry in Rome:

> Yesterday evening the twenty-fourth at ten pm excavations at Pompeii were hit by three bombs during an aerial attack on the neighbouring towns of the Vesuvius region. One fell on the forum, one on the House of Romulus and Remus, causing substantial damage; a third fell on the Antiquarium causing serious damage to archaeological objects, only some of which will be able to be restored. As aerial bombardments will continue and become heavier I think it's necessary to request neutral states to intervene to stop the blind and brutal bombing that threatens to destroy Pompeii, a sacred monument of the whole of civilisation. I personally took a close look at the damage to the site and have taken measures for restoration. I'd like to report that the behaviour of the guards on night shift was exemplary.[23]

At this point Maiuri had no idea that this was just the beginning. Allied intelligence assumed that the German troops who'd occupied Italy after the fall of Hitler's ally Benito Mussolini were using the excavation sites as shelters and weapons stores. After the landing this information would turn out to be false.

Until the arrival of the Allied forces on 29 September 1943 more than 170 bombs fell on Pompeii. Particularly badly hit were those places closest to the sea between Porta Marina and Porto Ercolano. But even inland buildings such as the House of Loreius Tiburtinus or the House of Venus in the Shell were badly hit. Maiuri did what he could to bring portable artefacts to safety, sustaining a leg injury during the course of the bombardments.

Traces of the bombs are still visible today. In the House of the Faun a piece of bomb shrapnel was left visible in the side atrium as a reminder. In 2021 excavations begun in the House of the Library revealed bomb craters in the mosaic floors. In one of the mosaics belonging to the neighbouring house there was a saying, like a warning to us descendants. *Ligitare noli*, it reads: 'don't argue!' What many people don't know is that the *Schola Armaturarum* – the building that collapsed in 2010, triggering an international scandal that was crucial for the subsequent salvage operation as part of the Great Pompeii Project – was also a victim of bombing in the Second World War. This was certainly not the only reason for its collapse, but it undoubtedly played a role.

Although the Villa of the Mysteries faces the sea, it was spared, not through any intervention by neutral states but probably by chance. On the evening of 18 September some bombs fell in the immediate vicinity of the villa. That the unique frieze could have been destroyed doesn't bear thinking about. Given all the destruction wrought by the bombs in Pompeii, for Maiuri too this might have been a ray of light in the darkness. For in a sense he was the man who discovered the villa. This may sound strange considering that the room with the Dionysian frieze, the highlight of the entire complex, was excavated back in 1909–10, fifteen years before Maiuri took up his post at Pompeii.

But discovery in archaeology is a story in itself. Seldom or never is it the work of an individual; archaeology is teamwork. Think of a statue lying in the ground. From the worker or student on excavation fieldwork, who literally takes it out of the ground, to the supervisor responsible for a specific area, to the professor or director, who might only stop by the site every few days but has masterminded the dig and obtained the funding for it – who deserves the credit for being the person who discovered the statue? And what about those cases where the real discovery only takes place years or decades after the excavation?

In partnership with universities and research centres, we're currently cataloguing thousands of finds in Pompeii that were dug out of the ground ages ago; in many cases the excavators have since died. Here the actual discovery is not so much the moment when an object, be it a statuette, coin or shard of pottery, is taken from the ground and plonked in a box, encrusted with earth, unrestored and virtually unrecognisable. It's much more the moment when the object is cleaned, examined and put into a broader context. Only then can it disclose the information that tells us about its significance.

The discovery of the Villa of the Mysteries is similar, albeit on a much larger scale. On 29 April 1909 one Aurelio Item, equipped with official state authorisation, began the excavation on his private property and soon came across the room with the

CAPTIVATING RITUALS

Dionysian frescoes. The works were carried out rapidly and without today's careful documentation of the sequence of layers, taking less than two weeks. On 16 May they were finished. A second excavation lasted from October 1909 to January 1910, when the authorisation expired. By the end only a really small portion of the villa, in addition to the Room of the Mysteries, was unearthed, a fact that paved the way for all manner of speculation over the original context of the frieze.

And so the Room of the Mysteries, which caused an immediate sensation, even outside of the archaeological community, was subject to the most controversial interpretations over the following years. The frieze is like a piece of a jigsaw puzzle, a beautiful one for sure, but the rest of the puzzle is missing. You can conceive of all manner of puzzles into which the piece would fit, but all this remains purely theoretical.

An initial summary analysis of the frieze came from the pen of the then director of Pompeii, Giulio De Petra. He'd come under fire for private excavations of ancient villas in the area surrounding Pompeii, for which he was even removed from his post between 1900 and 1906. He was accused of having been too casual about private excavations that had led to the sale of valuable finds and frescoes abroad. Some of these treasures still adorn the galleries of the Louvre or the Metropolitan Museum of Art in New York.

In the same year that the Villa of the Mysteries was discovered a law was passed prohibiting private excavations on Italian soil. The Villa of the Mysteries, first named 'Villa Item' after the owner of the land, marked a watershed in Italian heritage conservation. Here the state had to prove that it could do it better than private individuals, something we can also read between the lines of Maiuri's comprehensive 1931 work about the villa. The aim was not only to preserve the ancient buildings in their entirety and subject them to scholarly analysis, instead of plundering them and flogging the finds across the globe (often filling in the remaining ruins again afterwards), but also to ensure that the country villas surrounding Pompeii were made accessible and communicable to the public.

The Villa of the Mysteries thus launched a debate that continues today and which we will encounter again during the course of this book. On one side we have private individuals plundering ancient villas on their land – nowadays illegally of course, often using underground tunnel systems – to sell frescoes and other discoveries on the international art market. On the other side there are the authorities, who obviously have to stop such activity. At the same time, however, I believe it has the obligation to open up wider horizons. If we as a society invest in heritage conservation and research, what can heritage conservation and research give back to society?

Maiuri recognised this issue and clearly knew how to communicate it too. As he wrote gratefully in the foreword to his publication, the excavations between 1929 and 1930, which unearthed almost the entire villa, were financed by a bank, the Banco di Napoli. To my knowledge this is the first sponsor in the modern sense in the history of the excavations of Pompeii. When in 2014 the reform of the Italian museum sector not only allowed foreign directors to be appointed for the first time, but also introduced new conditions for such forms of cultural financing, it was possible to look back at a more than eighty-year-old precedent. After the loss of ticket revenue that the archaeological park of Pompeii suffered during the COVID-19 pandemic, work with private sponsors is now more important than ever.

However, along with accounting law, human resources management and communication, fundraising is one of those things that my generation didn't even remotely touch upon in our studies. Indeed, it's a fairly new feature of the Italian museum sector; Maiuri's pioneering work in the Villa of the Mysteries remained an isolated case for a long time.

When I came to Paestum in late 2015, it was like leaping into the water without having learned how to swim, not just for me but for the fundraising department that we conjured out of nothing. At my first event in the Paestum museum, a reading of ancient texts, the audience included one of the local mozzarella producers (Paestum is the original home of mozzarella).

After the reading I went straight up to him, saying that we urgently needed to renovate the room containing the famous Tomb of the Diver as there were huge holes in the carpet; financial help would be most welcome. He looked at me briefly and asked what the entire project would cost. I said €50,000. He replied that he'd work out if he could finance the whole thing. Later he admitted that he'd already taken the decision – it had been a gut feeling.

Outside experts helped us to familiarise ourselves with the area of fundraising, confirming more or less what we'd already found out: that trust and personal contact are key. It's about communicating values the backer can identify with and through which they can share in a project. But it also means opening up the museum, being transparent, making clear where there are shortcomings and where help will bring tangible results. If you ask for donations, you can't do it from the high horse that some in the culture industry like to sit on. Fundraising is thus also about the attitude an institution takes towards people – all the time, for if an attitude is to be authentic you can't put it on like a cloak. The higher the values incorporated by an institution – cultural, social, ethical – the more interesting it becomes to potential sponsors. For example, we haven't yet obtained a single cent for working with people with disabilities, who represent a priority in Pompeii. And yet without these projects, which also required a certain change in thinking from the museum staff, we would probably have had less support overall from the private sector.

Compared to, say, US museums, which finance most of their budgets from private donations, the sums we generally raise are not exorbitant. But it's a start. And even small contributions from the region are important because, unlike tax revenue, they represent a conscious desire to become involved.

CAPTIVATING RITUALS

The first analysis of the Villa of the Mysteries by De Petra made the frieze instantly famous. But what is there to see in it? Many archaeologists believe that we should read the frieze as a single coherent composition that, looking towards the door, starts on the right-hand (north) wall and runs clockwise around the entire room, interrupted by a large window in the south wall and the two entrances. Depicted are young women in various stages of a ritual. A boy reading (prayers, maybe?) and sacrificial offerings are the subject of the north wall, while the central east wall shows – under the gaze of Dionysus himself, enthroned beside a female companion (Ariadne or Semele) – the imminent uncovering of an object hidden beneath a cloth (a typical element of various mystery rituals). Painted on the south wall are ritual flagellation and naked – in other words wild Dionysian – dancing. On the other half of this wall and on both sides of the west wall are a bride preparing for her wedding, accompanied by Cupids, and a matron sitting on a chair.

Apart from the object being uncovered, probably the sculpture of an erect penis, a typical Dionysian symbol, the ritual flagellation is reminiscent of a Dionysian rite. The ancient writer Pausanias, who travelled to Greece in the second century CE, mentions a temple of Dionysus in Alea in the Peloponnese where 'every year a festival by the name of Skiereia is celebrated and on this occasion, at the bidding of an oracle from Delphi, women are flagellated'.[24] Likewise, ecstatic dancing to flutes and cymbals, as portrayed on the frieze, is characteristic of Dionysian rites in which women and men enter a trance. Wine, Dionysus's chief attribute, plays a key role here. The way in which the god slouches on his throne in the centre of the frieze suggests that he isn't quite sober either. But the power of music ought not to be underestimated. It's no coincidence that all manner of musical instruments appear in the mystery frieze. Besides the cymbals in the hands of the dancers, lyres and panpipes are being played. Nor is it coincidence that, in his First Epistle to the Corinthians, St Paul uses Dionysian cymbals (*kymbala*) as a metaphor for meaningless religiosity when referring to the hollowness of pagan rites. As far as Christians were concerned, the Dionysian cult must have been perceived as a potential rival.

It wasn't only Christianity that struggled with Dionysus. As mentioned above, Euripides's *The Bacchae* shows that already in classical Greece the cult of Dionysus encountered resistance. How much more difficult it must have been with the morally stricter Romans. As we saw in the previous chapter, their relationship to Greek culture had always been ambivalent. This is reflected in the pantheon of gods too. Whereas Apollo, god of harmony and truth, had been easily adopted by Rome back in the fifth century BCE, Dionysus's integration into Rome and Italy was a seriously complex and protracted process.

Unlike Apollo, who kept his Greek name in Rome, Dionysus was identified with an archaic fertility god, but one with specifically Roman features: Liber, literally 'the free one', associated with the goddess of the fields, Ceres. As a couple, Liber and Ceres inhabit a different domain of course from Dionysus and Ariadne. We are in the sphere of traditional agricultural cults that have little in common with the innovative, sometimes visionary nature of the 'new god' and his originally mortal partner Ariadne. Moreover, Liber, as one of the so-called plebeian

Triad of Liber, Ceres and Libera (a feminine form of Liber), has social connotations. He is a god of the *plebs*, the common people. This too differentiates him from the Greek Dionysus, who was also popular with the people but whose cult in Athens, Thebes and other cities was very much a matter for the establishment elite.

The tension between Dionysus, often called Bacchus in Latin, and traditional Roman religion ultimately culminated in a veritable scandal, during the course of which heads rolled, both because of death sentences passed by Roman courts as well as the suicides of men and women caught up in it. The chronicle of the scandal, which appears in book 39 of Livy's history of Rome, reads like a crime novel. It is 186 BCE. A dangerous sect has spread through Rome and Italy, beginning with an 'anonymous Greek who'd moved to Etruria'. The night-time ritual, which originally was restricted to women (described as 'bacchanale' after Bacchus), is opened up to men after the intervention of a priestess from Campania. Soon it embraces all classes of society, from slaves to the Roman high aristocracy.

The story contains all the elements we're used to seeing in articles about pseudo-gurus that keep cropping up in today's media. The religion is just an excuse; in truth it's about sex and money. Seals and testaments are falsified for the sake of personal enrichment. Young men are initiated into the cult to exploit them sexually and extort money from them. Those who don't play along or even threaten to leave are summarily murdered (the screams of the victims, Livy wrote, were drowned out by 'drums and cymbals'). But most of all, with their night-time music and wine, the Bacchic rites degenerate into real orgies in which not only men and women fall on each other, but also – by Roman standards extremely problematic – same-sex intercourse takes place between free citizens.

The mystery nature of the rites makes it easier to keep things secret; the initiates are convinced that if they reveal anything of what happens they are violating divine law. Only a chance occurrence eventually leads to one of the two Roman consuls in 186 BCE, Postumius, finding out what's going on. By Livy's estimation more than 7,000 men and women had already been initiated into the cult, some from the highest circles. The Senate, which Postumius addresses, is horrified. The initiation of young men causes particular concern. Should youths tainted like this, Postumius asks the assembled senators, become Roman soldiers? The consul doesn't fail to point out that we can't talk of religion in the traditional sense here, and thus any religious misgivings should be cast aside. When the state is in peril, piety stops, especially if, according to Postumius, we're talking about a *prava religio*, a 'perverted religion'. 'Nothing is more dangerous!' he says.

The reaction of the Roman authorities is correspondingly severe, even though many of the victims of the persecution that now ensues are themselves from the Roman upper class:

> The number of those executed exceeded those imprisoned, and ran to an enormous number of men and women from both classes. The women found guilty were handed over to their relatives or guardians for private punishment; if there was nobody to mete out the punishment they were publicly executed. The next task of the consuls was to suppress all the

Bacchus cults, first in Rome then in the whole of Italy. Only long-standing altars and sacred images were excepted. The Senate issued a decree saying that Bacchus cults were no longer permitted to exist either in Rome or in Italy.[25]

A bronze plaque with a transcript of the Senate's decree, *de Bacchanalibus* ('on Bacchus cults/rites'), was discovered in 1640 in the small Calabrian town of Tiriolo; today it is kept in Vienna's Kunsthistorisches Museum.

The text of the bacchanale decree expressly stated that the prohibition applied to both the private and the public spheres. That would appear to settle the interpretation of the mystery frieze discovered in Pompeii. Theoretically the prohibition issued in 186 BCE was still in force in the first century BCE, when the frieze was painted. Does this then mean that the room with the mystery frieze was a private chapel in which the old rites continued to be celebrated despite the ban? A secret room outside the gates of the city where the adepts of the Bacchus cult gathered at night for their rites, similar to the Christians later in the catacombs outside the gates of Rome? And assuming this to be the case, is the frieze to be read as a coded message, a sort of Dionysian confession of faith that presented the secret content of the induction cult to the initiates at their gatherings?

The decades following the discovery of the room with the frieze were particularly receptive to these questions. In light of the abuses of modern capitalism and even more so the senseless mass slaughter of the First World War, belief in the rationalism of the Enlightenment had unravelled. What is the value of Enlightenment rationalism, many people asked at the time, if it leads to the killing fields of war and death by starvation, or at least is unable to prevent these?

In the first half of the twentieth century new forms of expression in art, but in spirituality too (think, for example, of anthroposophy), highlighted the boundaries of rational thought and re-evaluated the irrational and supernatural.

Art history and archaeology were not unaffected by this development. Although for the time being most archaeologists had little use for the symbolist paintings of Gustav Klimt or Picasso's cubist pictures, they were also in search of new patterns of interpretation for what appeared long familiar. Mystical and symbolic interpretations were in vogue; the discovery of the Dionysian frieze occurred at a time that seemed to have been ripe for such a work of art.

Maiuri reacted to this development with scepticism. As the son of a public prosecutor in provincial southern Italy, he remained attached to an enlightened humanism. This would also prevent him from becoming too closely connected to another expression of the new irrationalism: Fascism. Although Maiuri continued to work in positions of responsibility in Naples and Pompeii throughout the era of Italian Fascism (1922–43), following the Second World War he was able to resume his work after a brief hiatus.

CAPTIVATING RITUALS

What irritated the detail-loving archaeologist and excavator most of all were the overly speculative intellectual interpretations, even though the plan of the building that housed the Room of the Mysteries wasn't yet known. Fantastic theories were penned about secret cult chapels while the room was still an isolated fragment of a complex yet to be excavated – and which risked being damaged by weather, inaccessibility and inadequate preservation. There was not even a proper photographic record or other illustrated documentation of the find of the century.

The new excavations that would make Maiuri a 'second-level discoverer' of the Villa of the Mysteries were intended as a response to the problems outlined above, as Maiuri made clear in his publication about the 1932 excavations: improving the preservation conditions, creating the appropriate documentation and clarifying how the frieze fits spatially, historically and culturally into its surroundings.[26]

Looking back, we can say that all these goals were achieved. To my mind, Maiuri's 'Operation Villa of the Mysteries' is a textbook example of the interplay between research, monument conservation and cultural mediation. It's thanks to Maiuri that the villa is nowadays part of the visitor itinerary at Pompeii. The reconstruction of the roofs especially is a result of his engagement, even if some of this work only took place after his time.

For example, in the atrium, the central courtyard, we can admire the ancient roof with its characteristic opening – the impluvium – as a reconstruction. Not only does this protect the frescoes and mosaics from the weather, it also gives visitors an idea of spatiality, acoustics and the incidence of light in a 2,000-year old building. We wouldn't use concrete beams today, as was the usual practice after the war (Maiuri's first restoration used wooden beams, just as they had in antiquity), because the heavy concrete elements lead to all sorts of problems and are less durable than was once hoped. The basic principles applied here, however – reconstruction of the ancient roof structure, but identifiable to all as a modern addition – are still used today for the restoration of archaeological monuments.

Maiuri remains an unavoidable presence for anyone conducting research into the villa. By exposing almost the entire complex he gave the frieze back its original context. I say 'almost' because a small section that faces the ancient access road continues to resist excavation. This part wasn't expropriated and remained in private hands; the owners built a small house and garden on it that was occupied until 2020. Only then was the park able to purchase the property, and over the coming years we will finally be able to complete the excavation that Maiuri began. Before that, however, the modern house will have to be demolished.

We have already seen with the Apollo statue from the House of the Citharist how important context is for archaeology. The term 'context' comes originally from linguistics and everyone is familiar with its meaning. 'You look really hot,' one seven-year-old can say innocently to another if they are red in the face. A few years later that phrase has acquired a totally different meaning.

It's similar with the Room of the Mysteries. Only when we know in which 'text' the 'phrase' is set – i.e. which architectural context the room with the frieze is embedded in – does its meaning become accessible. Maiuri's conclusions after the excavations were finished leave no room for doubt. He says the complex is a typical suburban villa, while the Room of the Mysteries (Maiuri calls it '*oecus*') fits perfectly into a category of living rooms facing the sea that we find both in the same villa and in many other Roman villas. Moreover, the room is directly connected by a door to a bedroom with two alcoves (bed niches), which is also decorated with Dionysian themes. This was clearly one of the bedrooms used by the paterfamilias and his wife, depending on the time of year.

Let's read what Maiuri has to say about this:

> Alcoves and *oecus* thus formed a uniform complex within the grand rooms of the villa. Merely on the basis of the two plans we drew up of the pre-Roman and Roman phases, it's impossible to seriously suggest that these rooms in the southwest wing of the villa were isolated from the rest for the purposes of secret, occult religious ceremonies or even that they were a sort of chapel or a meeting place for the members of an exotic religion proscribed by the state. For both the room with the alcoves and the 'oecus' open onto the atrium and from there to the terraces and garden. No mystery, of whatever sort, could envelop this room, which was designed to enjoy a magnificent and extensive view of the countryside, mountains and sea, while its broad door and large window could not have protected it from the indiscreet eyes of slaves and other members of the household.[27]

Another, simpler explanation of the frieze is needed. Maiuri also gives us this in his book, after a thorough analysis. The topic is Dionysian, certainly, but with an important idiosyncrasy. The women of various ages in the centre of the rites should be seen as brides and matrons, and the rites should be viewed as linked to the initiation of young women in preparation for marriage. Indeed, given the private family context of the room, it's likely that the marriage of the owner and his bride was the reason to decorate it with a theme we know played an important role for women of the upper class. For, Maiuri argues, although the ban of 186 BCE was to our knowledge never lifted, countless examples, especially in Campania, showed that Dionysian cult associations and priesthoods had blossomed again. In the Bacchus cult there were also priestesses who usually came from the eminent families of the city; the mistress of the Villa of the Mysteries was probably one of these. In short, the frieze shows mystery rituals, not for a secret cult community, but as a conspicuous decoration to welcome the newly wed mistress who was perhaps a Dionysian priestess herself.[28]

Not only did Maiuri put the discussion about the mystery frieze on a whole new footing, he also proved his greatness in another field. He made no secret of the fact that his interpretation of the frieze had in many points been pre-empted by a colleague of his: Margarete Bieber, who had already identified the theme of marriage – from the bride's perspective – as the central subject of the frieze.²⁹

Margarete Bieber, born on 31 July 1879 in Schönau in West Prussia (now Przechowo in Poland), was one of the first women to gain a PhD in Classical Archaeology at a German university. She also progressed to get her licence to teach at university, becoming the first woman to be awarded a postdoctoral qualification in Archaeology and the third woman to get it overall in Germany. The travel grant from the German Archaeological Institute was another first. Since 1859 it has been awarded to outstanding graduates in Archaeology, allowing them to visit archaeological sites around the world without any obligation to produce academic output such as articles or books. All they have to do is travel to and view ancient sites and museums. As someone who was privileged to receive this grant I can only emphasise how important it is, especially in our achievement-obsessed era, to preserve this opportunity for apparently unproductive travel and learning. Even today I'm still drawing on the impressions, discoveries and experiences of those six months that took me around the eastern Mediterranean.

It took Bieber two attempts to obtain the grant, merely because she was a woman. In her memoirs she recalls that one of the chairmen of the German Archaeological Institute, Ernst Fabricius, was supposed to have said when she first applied in 1908 that so long as he was director 'no woman will ever receive a grant!'³⁰ The following year, however, her application was successful, although resistance remained. The description of her meeting with the other 1909 fellows in Athens is instructive:

When the fellows arrived I soon realised that I was going to be ostracised. They stuck together the whole time and nobody took any notice of me. I decided to leave the institute and move into a guesthouse. Eventually the youngest and most talented of my colleagues, Rodenwaldt, broke the ice and paid me a visit. I received him cordially, invited him for coffee and cake and, as he could sing German songs and play the piano, I rented one. We had lovely musical evenings together as well as good scholarly discussions. Then the rest came, one by one, to pay their respects. They were invited to the music evenings and soon we were a nice little family. I was the mother of five adopted sons. From that point on they wouldn't travel without me. We took trips throughout Greece and they showered me with attentiveness.[31]

Bieber also met with rejection in Miletus, where she visited the excavations being undertaken by the German Archaeological Institute. Although she was given a friendly reception by the head of the dig, Wilhelm Dörpfeld, Professor Erich Pernice, who was taking part in the excavations, noted in his diary: 'the presence of Fräulein Bieber was particularly ghastly'. Evidently some men were horrified by the idea of a female scholar visiting a dig.

During the First World War, when research assistants were called up by the dozen for military service, Bieber's mentor Gerhard Loeschke brought her to Berlin University (now the Humboldt University) as a stand-in lecturer. But when Loeschke's successor, Ferdinand Noack, took the helm, he was, as Bieber recalled, 'furious at having found a woman there'. Not only did this put an end to her teaching, Noack also barred Bieber from using the institute's academic facilities and collections.[32]

The portraits of these men – Loeschke, Noack, Rodenwaldt – still adorned the Berlin Institute of Classical Archaeology when I studied there in the 2000s. But you would search in vain for a portrait of Margarete Bieber. It was only after my time as a student, almost a century after Bieber's first lectures, that the first woman was appointed Professor of Classical Archaeology at the Humboldt University.

Maiuri's appreciation of Bieber's work was thus most valuable for her efforts at professional recognition. Until she secured a chair in Giessen she had to put up with a number of further setbacks, some humiliating. Quite a few male colleagues lacked Maiuri's authority and hid their misogyny behind disparaging comments about Bieber's academic achievements, which meanwhile were being increasingly acknowledged internationally.

When she finally made it, in 1933, she was dismissed before she could even officially take up the post at Giessen because of her Jewish background. In America she started from scratch again, having to struggle against prejudice there too. In 1978 she died in New Canaan, Connecticut. As late as 1977 – at the age of ninety-eight! – she received a grant from the National Endowment for the Humanities, thereby breaking yet another record.

It's a pity that one of the more recent publications on the Villa of the Mysteries mentions Bieber only in passing, even though the work is based on her approach. In a book published in 2016 the French archaeologist and historian Paul Veyne argued that the real subject of the frieze was marriage from the bride's perspective.[33] According to Veyne, it couldn't be about Dionysian mysteries. At most, he conceded, there were humorous allusions, but definitely no references to mystery cults that deserved to be taken seriously. The basket with the hidden object on the eastern wall was the only certain clue to Dionysian mysteries in the entire frieze. What's depicted is the grain sifter, *liknon* in Greek, hidden in which was a phallus. In the rituals these two objects played a key role that is not precisely understood today. In any event, Veyne contends that it is a mere allegory. The discovery of the hidden penis-shaped sculpture in the sifter by the young woman is an allusion to her losing her virginity on her wedding night.

Dionysus is not depicted in his role as a mystery god, but as a popular patron of sensual pleasure, fertility and prosperity. It is not mystical piety speaking from the frieze but overflowing joie de vivre, mixed with double meaning and humour. Thus the satyrs and sileni, the pointy-eared wood spirits from Dionysus's retinue, here embody the male wedding guests with music and drink. A maenad, who's giving her breast to a kid, should – according to Veyne – be seen as an allegory of a mother invited to the wedding who has brought her infant along.

What might at first appear strange, Veyne explains, point by point, using comparable examples from the ancient world. He

CAPTIVATING RITUALS

focuses particularly on the comparison of the mystery frieze with a fresco preserved in the Vatican Museums, known as the 'Aldobrandini Wedding'.

The parallels that Veyne reveals run into inconspicuous details. For example, he refers to a writing tablet in an oddly upright position on the armrest of the 'matron's' chair, the matron being the mother of the bride to the right of the door. According to Veyne, this is the marriage contract. A similar tablet can be found on the fresco in the Vatican Museums. In Pompeii a number of such tablets have been found, in an outstanding state of preservation considering that they're made out of wood. Most of them contained lease and purchase contracts; in some cases there were IOUs too.

Paul Veyne presents his thesis, supported by a wealth of detail, as 'heretical'. In fact, he's reinforcing what Margarete Bieber was suggesting back in 1928: no mysteries, merely an original depiction of a wedding, wrapped in places in humorous allegory. The scene was painted from the bride's viewpoint, but by men for men, who maybe were laughing at the virgin shocked by the penis in the grain sifter under the cloth. Such macho jokes were typical of ancient humour.

Veyne suggests that a better name for the Villa of the Mysteries would be the 'Marriage Villa'. Talking of the mysteries, Veyne devotes an entire chapter to them, merely to show that they didn't play any role worth mentioning. Mysteries, he argues, had little to do with orgies, philosophy or spirituality. Most of all, however, the hope for life after death, often seen as a parallel to the Christian religion, is totally overvalued. It's only a side issue, he insists. And so, Veyne concludes, the mystery cults 'did not anticipate Christianity with its "mysteries" and its quite distinct religiousness, unless you assume that when it comes to the topic of "mysticism" everything is one and the same'.[34]

Which brings us back to the restaurant in Paris and Gabriella's objection. Is anyone who sees mysteries here being taken in, perhaps, by their Western–Christian predisposition?

My first response to this would be that the role of death in ancient mystery cults is only seemingly a peripheral issue. Certainly the talk isn't always of death, but essentially everything revolves around it. According to mystic tradition, Dionysus is the god who is torn to pieces, eaten and resurrected. The mystery of life arises from human mortality and the possibility of overcoming this.

Second, I would turn the argument around and ask whether the attempt by Veyne and others to make a clean break between Christianity and mystery cults, simply to exclude any parallels between the two, isn't subconsciously more Christian than the supposedly Christian-influenced interpretation of the frieze as a depiction of mysteries. Is this attempt to present Christianity as a special religion that has nothing in common with the other contemporaneous mystery cults not part of a tradition that has always been keen to characterise the Christian religion as something unique and standing outside of history? To decouple it from the history of the ancient Mediterranean and bestow it with the universal historical, global significance that it claims for itself as an absolute, divine truth?

Many churchgoers might not wish to hear that Jesus's message is related to Dionysian orgies or Isis the healer. And in his harsh rejection of any analogy between Christianity and mystery cults, maybe Paul Veyne too was subconsciously following an impulse from his childhood in Catholic Aix-en-Provence. For the avoidance of any misunderstanding, I've never met Paul Veyne personally and I have no objective reason to suppose this. It is merely the question about our internal engines that prompts such speculation (for it is nothing more than this . . .) as well as the suspicion that others too make their way through academic life with an engine buried deep inside.

Veyne provides a subtle clue to his engine, moreover, in one of his chapter headings: 'A Dionysian summer day's dream'. From beneath the academically sound bonnet of arguments and data, here the sound of the engine comes through. For me, reading Veyne's book meant understanding the mystery frieze not as a mystic tragedy but as a Shakespearean comedy. Or, more accurately, to view the frieze with background music that is more akin to Mendelssohn's setting of Shakespeare's *A Midsummer Night's Dream* than the fateful tones of Brahms's 'German Requiem', say. Here too I don't know to what extent my impression overlaps with the author's personal motivation. At any rate I found Veyne's book compelling – I devoured it in two days – and it gave a boost to my own academic motor. This doesn't mean I'm convinced by all his arguments. On the contrary, I have a different opinion on many points. But the man can drive and takes the reader on an enjoyable spin.

The same is true for one of his compatriots, the archaeologist Gilles Sauron, who published a book on the mystery frieze in 1998 that goes to the other extreme.[35] Sauron pulls out all the stops to assert the mystic interpretation of the frieze. The two texts can be read as a sort of dialogue or debate. Or as a concert featuring the music of both Brahms and Mendelssohn – you can prefer one without despising the other.

It's like this in archaeology too. Our interpretations are attempts to get close to a complex reality that has long since passed. To fixate dogmatically on one specific reading is the biggest mistake you can make. For Sauron substantiates his theory with arguments that are no less detailed and sophisticated than Veyne's. Here's just one example of many. The couple in the middle of the north wall are usually understood to be Dionysus and Ariadne; Sauron's interpretation is that they're Dionysus and Semele, the god's mother. Part of his reasoning is that the female figure is precisely in the middle axis of the picture, whereas Dionysus is literally standing or lying 'beneath her'. Such a hierarchical relationship in the image, according to Sauron, doesn't tally with the lovers Dionysus and Ariadne, but definitely works for a depiction of a mother with her son. And if you look carefully, he observes, you can see that just below the gap where the upper part of Semele/Ariadne has sadly disappeared, the hand of the woman sitting is visible, clutching the corner of a cloth. This gesture, as Sauron shows using comparable examples, is typical of maternal figures, so-called matrons, making sure that their veil doesn't flap away.

CAPTIVATING RITUALS

Seriously? Is archaeology still unable to give a clear answer after more than a century since the discovery of the frieze? No, it's not. Maybe future discoveries of similar images will give us clarity, or maybe the discussion will go on for another century.

This doesn't mean that we should give up our aspiration for objectivity. But objectivity, at least in the humanities, is never the privilege of an individual. It comes from considered discussions, the back and forth of arguments, scholarly duels such as that between Veyne and Sauron where nobody gets badly hurt, but everyone learns a lot.

And behind all of this you can hear the engines humming, driving each and every one of us to throw us into the fray and join the debate. From my own experience this is how I would describe it. An academic book or article often starts with a flash of intuition, as may well have been the case with Paul Veyne when he saw the mystery frieze: What if we set all of this to Mendelssohn's 'A Midsummer Night's Dream'? The arguments come afterwards. A word of caution here. This doesn't mean that as a scholar you can allow yourself to be led by your feelings. Borne, yes, but not led. If the arguments suddenly point in a different direction, you can turn around and be borne somewhere else.

Try it out for yourself – thanks to smartphones it's really quite simple these days. Stand in front of the mystery frieze in Pompeii and choose the soundtrack that you feel best goes with it. Brahms, Mendelssohn, Bach, Mozart . . . or Thelonius Monk, Pink Floyd, Bob Marley, Billie Eilish . . . Creativity knows no bounds. And who knows, perhaps your personal soundtrack will turn out to be the basis of a new reading of the frieze. This would, of course, have to be tested by argument.

CHAPTER THREE
A CITY ON THE VERGE OF CATASTROPHE

Rome, one hot day in June 2022. The meeting point is a workshop that opens onto a narrow street on the left bank of the Tiber, barely larger than a garage. Door and windows are secured with thick iron bars, because this is no ordinary workshop but a conservation laboratory. And inside it a most unusual find is being restored: a ceremonial carriage, excavated from a villa in Civita Giuliana, not far from Pompeii, in early 2021. It was Massimo Osanna's last great discovery before he moved to become Director General of museums and parks at the Ministry of Culture in Rome. We're meeting today to get an update on the progress of the work and to discuss possible ways of exhibiting the carriage, for the object is in a hundred pieces that only make sense as parts of a whole.

How can these fragile fragments of bronze, iron and wood be reassembled to make the carriage comprehensible to the public? Virtually on a screen or 'in real life'? Should the missing pieces of wood, leather and textiles be replaced using the same materials? Or would this confuse the public as they wouldn't know what was original and what reconstructed? Might it therefore be better to replace the missing bits with Plexiglas? Or would that prove even more problematic, making the whole thing look more like a spaceship than an ancient carriage?

When it was discovered in February 2021 the carriage was an international sensation. Once again the particular conditions in Pompeii had ensured that much had been preserved that elsewhere would have decomposed, such as leather and wood, or recycled, as often happened with metal. On that fateful day in 79 CE the carriage, ready for harnessing, was buried in a layer of ash that filled the courtyard of the villa outside the walls of Pompeii. During the excavation it had to be disassembled. The exact position of even the smallest component was precisely documented with a laser scanner. This was important, not only so the carriage could be reconstructed later, but also to understand exactly how it worked, from the suspension to the seat padding. These are banal aspects of ancient everyday life, which are often more obscure to us than the sublime philosophy and art of the time. We know much about the philosophical ideas spinning around Seneca's head, but astonishingly little about the mechanism that prevented him from getting a sore bottom while taking a carriage ride.

Another particularity of the carriage is the decoration: it's covered all over with bronze and silver reliefs, many of them sporting erotic motifs. Maenads and satyrs are either moving in on each other or they're already riotously getting down to business. Such a richly ornate vehicle certainly wasn't just for getting from A to B. Like a Ferrari, it was as much a status symbol as a vehicle for getting around in. In actual fact the carriage is a status symbol. It's likely that on the day when it was in the courtyard, ready for harnessing, some ceremony was planned for which such a vehicle would have been used. Then Vesuvius threw a spanner in the works.

Massimo's theory is that the carriage had been prepared for a wedding ceremony. In ancient weddings the bride's journey from her parents' house to her new home played a key role. More than contracts and words, this ritual transfer made clear that the woman now belonged to her husband's household.[36]

For this reason the Villa of the Mysteries, alias the Wedding Villa, is also floating around our heads on that summer's day in Rome. Are there parallels between the frieze and the reliefs decorating the carriage? As I have said, the popular interpretation has Dionysus and Ariadne at the centre of the frieze. Does the couple, immortal god and mortal woman, appear on the carriage too? This wouldn't be proof, but it would be another lead to bolster the marriage thesis for both the Villa of the Mysteries and Civita Giuliana.

That day something new comes to light. Not a 'discovery' exactly, but one of those mosaic tessera that slowly produce a picture. As we've seen, the discovery continues after the excavation; indeed, sometimes that's where it really begins.

On the back of the carriage were three large medallions with reliefs made of silver-plated lead. The two on either side depict erotic scenes, but the middle one had previously been illegible. The high temperature of the pyroclastic wave melted the lead and made it clump together with the ash and dust. Now the painstakingly detailed work of the restorers has revealed an initial detail: a face turned to the left, framed by the right, bent arm.

This gesture is typical of Dionysian imagery. With a similarly angled arm the drunken god is depicted in relief on a large krater, a vessel for mixing wine and water, which was found in a grave at Deveni in northern Greece. But the gesture is even more typical of Ariadne when she is discovered by Dionysus, asleep, abandoned on the island of Naxos. We encountered this motif in the first chapter, along with the variation that turns the female Ariadne into a hermaphrodite, very much to the astonishment of her male discoverer. For the time being this is a working hypothesis, but one thing is certain: the discovery is still going on. Not only in the laboratory, but also at the excavation site, for the villa at Civita Giuliana is far from having been fully explored.

It's not just the care taken by archaeologists as they uncover and document such fascinating finds as the ceremonial carriage that prevents the villa from being explored quickly. Legal and even criminal reasons are at play too.

What would turn out to be a real archaeological crime story had its beginnings in a 2017 investigation by the public prosecutor's office in Torre Annunziata, whose jurisdiction also covers Pompeii. In the course of their inquiry, detectives came across a ring of thieves involved in large-scale looting of ancient villas surrounding Pompeii, then hawking their finds on the international black market. Collector syndrome ensures an ongoing demand. Those who get their hands dirty at the ancient site are only the bottom links in a chain stretching all the way up to the highest ranks of organised crime. After drugs, human trafficking and prostitution, the illegal trade in antiquities from archaeological looting is one of the most lucrative sectors for the Camorra, as the Neapolitan version of the mafia is called.

The quaint image of the moustachioed, patriarchal clan boss, as evoked in films and novels, has long been superseded by reality. Mafia organisations operate just as globally as hedge funds and international corporations. They exist throughout Europe, discreetly, often in the grey areas of legality. Income from human trafficking and drugs is invested in businesses and property in London, Paris and Berlin with the returns 'laundered' into the pockets of the organisation as legal wealth.

'Laundering' looted archaeological goods isn't always easy, but still easy enough because buyers often turn a blind eye. The looted object is given a sort of sham biography. 'Found in an attic in Switzerland' or 'Owned by a family for generations' are typical fabricated provenance descriptions for illegally excavated antiquities.

Another strategy is to claim that the item was found in international waters. This is highly improbable because national waters end twelve nautical miles from the coast, at which point the seabed is so deep almost everywhere that archaeological objects are virtually never salvaged and certainly not coincidentally by fishing boats, as is often claimed. But once the legend has been put out there, the opposite needs to be proved, which isn't always straightforward.

In Pompeii we've recently had one such case: a statue of the Doryphoros that ended up in the Minneapolis Institute of Art in Minnesota, USA. The Doryphoros, literally 'spear carrier', is one of the most famous works of classical Greek art. The sculptor Polykleitos made it around 440 BCE to show how the male body should be depicted – naked, obviously. The statue was thus originally described as the 'canon' (i.e. standard or model).

The bronze original hasn't survived, and so we know the Doryphoros only from Roman marble copies. They are not identical and all of them have gaps. Sometimes it's the head that's missing, sometimes an arm or a leg, sometimes only the torso has been preserved. To reconstruct the original, therefore, it's important to know lots of copies, ones that are as complete as possible, and then compare them. In archaeological jargon the German word *Kopienkritik* is often used to describe this.

The statue in Minneapolis is not only one of the best copies, it is also preserved almost completely. It's one of the most expensive too. At US$2.5 million, it's the costliest purchase the museum in Minneapolis has ever made.

The Americans were almost beaten to it by the Glyptothek in Munich, where the Doryphoros was exhibited in 1980. The statue was offered via Switzerland, supposedly having been found in international waters off the Italian coast in the 1930s. The masterpiece enticed the curators of the Munich collection of antiquities. To pay the exorbitant price they even launched a fundraising drive. Then came the sudden decision not to buy, ostensibly for cost reasons. In reality, however, rumours were already circulating, which reached the press, that there was something fishy about the find. And indeed the statue shows no traces of having been covered by shells or corrosion, which are typical of sculptures salvaged from salt water.

A CITY ON THE VERGE OF CATASTROPHE

Those responsible in Minneapolis at the time don't appear to have shared those concerns, even though they were seemingly aware of the rumours too. The Italian office of public prosecution came into the possession of correspondence in which the American curators allegedly write of the 'old Castellammare theft'. This doesn't mean that they knew all the details. At the time they claimed the authenticity of the sculpture had never been questioned. That was in 1986. Thirty-five years later the case was reopened when an Italian Court ruled that the statue was found in 1976 during construction works in Castellammare di Stabia, on the site of the ancient city of Stabiae, not far from Pompeii where the coast bends from the Sarno plain to the Sorrento Peninsula. At the time of the eruption of Vesuvius the city no longer existed, having been razed to the ground in the Social War of 91–89 BCE.

On the wonderful stretch of land that had housed this once important city, between the Campanian coast and the steep wooded slopes of Monte Faito, villas were built by rich Romans, one beside the other. The ancient geographer Strabo writes a few decades after the destruction of Stabiae that the coast of Campania was lined with an uninterrupted stretch of villas, 'as if it were one large city'.[37]

Some of the villas have been excavated and can be visited today. They are under the administration of the Archaeological Park of Pompeii. In the archaeological museum in Castellammare di Stabia, which also belongs to the park, frescoes and sculptures from the villas are on display. One of the goals of my work in Pompeii is to make these examples of ancient art better known. For the artistic quality of the paintings and sculptures from the villas of Stabiae exceeds that of what we know from most of the houses in Pompeii. The rich and super-rich lived here, which is reflected in the extravagance with which they decorated their villas.

The Doryphoros of Stabiae is a good example of this. It also makes clear why the surrounding area of Pompeii continues to whet the appetite of thieves and unscrupulous art dealers. Not only are there many unexplored villas outside the guarded and fenced area of the park, they are also potential gold mines for a market gasping for artistic treasures. The buyers, which sadly have included foreign museums, especially in the US, are indifferent to the fact that this leads to the destruction of the real treasure. After all, for archaeology the true worth of the frescoes and statues isn't their market value, but the contribution to knowledge that they afford us. To maximise this gain in knowledge, however, we have to know the context of a find, which looting of archaeological sites destroys, mostly for ever. A coin, for example, that is stolen from a grave could have revealed a story contained in this grave. When was it created, what was the social status of the person buried in it, what do the funerary objects say about ancient ideas about life after death? Even if the coin returns to archaeology from the black market, it usually can't answer these questions any longer.

The same is true of the Doryphoros of Stabiae. As a copy of a Greek original this statue tells us not only about the art of its sculptor Polykleitos, but also about the way in which the Romans adopted this centuries-old legacy. To understand this, it would be important to know the context in which it was displayed. Was the statue in a villa, a temple or in a public place?

A CITY ON THE VERGE OF CATASTROPHE

And if it was in a villa, whereabouts in the villa? Was it part of a collection that included other sculptures it was in dialogue with, so to speak? These are questions that are likely to remain unanswered. Nonetheless it would be important for the Doryphoros to return to Stabiae. After all, the villas of Stabiae with their decorative sculptures, which, unlike the city of Pompeii, were soon inhabited again after the catastrophe, are no less part of its history than Polykleitos and the art of classical Greece.

In Civita Giuliana the state foiled the trade in antiquities even as the excavations were in progress. But the loss is still considerable: experts at the Ministry of Culture have estimated the damage caused by improper excavation, the destruction of ancient architecture and furnishings, and the removal of frescoes and other finds as coming to almost €2 million.

And the biggest puzzle of all is still waiting to be solved. In the tapped telephone calls that led to the exposure of the illegal excavations in Civita Giuliana, there was talk of a *biga*, a two-wheeled chariot. Which means there must have been another one. It cannot be the ceremonial carriage discovered in 2021, as that one has four wheels and the robbers didn't see it, having dug their tunnel three centimetres away.

On a summer's day in 2021 we climb down to the refreshingly cool air at the ancient villa, six metres below the narrow road that runs past here, wedged between fields and houses. Beside the part of the courtyard where the carriage was found are three small, unplastered rooms. Next to these is a stable where the remains of two horses were uncovered. This must be the working part of the villa. The living quarters of the master and mistress of the house were on the other side of the modern road.

A few rooms were exposed as long ago as 1907–08, as part of a private excavation, similar to what happened at the start of the discovery of the Villa of the Mysteries. More rooms have been explored since 2017, during which time two victims of the eruption were also found: an elderly, well-dressed man and a younger one in a simple robe, perhaps his slave. Casts were made of both.

The rest of the villa lies, to a great extent, beneath the street and neighbouring buildings. Was the second vehicle the robber talked about on the phone hidden there too? On that summer's day in 2021 we try to get closer to the answer with the help of the fire brigade.

Grave robbers are ahead of us in the sense that they don't give two figs about safety measures in the workplace. Unlike us they don't dig from the top to the bottom, but use a network of underground tunnels, the entrance to which is in the cellar of the house they're living in, directly above the villa. The tunnels extend from there beneath neighbouring properties and the road, breaking through ancient walls to get from one room to the next, and usually running along the walls where frescoes are expected to be found. These frescoes are then recklessly removed.

When I peer into the dark tunnel leading from the excavation to the road I feel a faint shudder. The tunnels are so narrow that you can only go down them on all fours. Where they come close to fragile layers of lapilli there is a serious risk of collapse, especially beneath the road, along which cars and trucks trundle. These robbers need strong nerves.

For this reason it's not particularly easy to get an overview of the intricate network of corridors that robbers have created over many years, risking their own lives in the progress. The fire brigade and police help us to edge our way into the underground world, charting and measuring it. We don't find out much that's new today.

All the same, this summer's day will linger long in my memory. Because to get to the tunnel entrance we had to pass a room that hadn't been fully excavated and which opened onto the courtyard, exactly where the carriage had been parked. From here a narrow passage led to the system of tunnels. There was about a metre of ash left to excavate. We walked over it without sparing much thought for it. After all, the excavation of the two unremarkable neighbouring rooms had revealed little or nothing.

But we were utterly wrong. This one-metre-deep layer of ash in the room, which was only 16 square metres in size, was hiding the most fascinating discovery I've been part of in my life as an archaeologist so far. And I'm saying this as someone who was lucky enough to be there when yet another Greek temple in Paestum was uncovered – smaller than the three ones known so far, yes, but one that was preserved in its entirety from the foundations to the gable. This was in 2019 during restoration works of the Paestum city walls. Another unforgettable find deserving of its own book.

But what we found here was different, precisely because it wasn't a temple, grave or palace. Not even an impressive house. There was no trace of wall decoration or architectural ornamentation; just 16 square metres of everyday hardship. But there is also an attempt to defy hardship and to create a modicum of intimacy and cosiness in such a cramped space at the very bottom of the social ladder: three camp beds, a tiny window, and a chamber pot beneath one of the beds.

The particular preservation conditions in Pompeii, thanks to which we also have casts of the victims of the volcano, had conserved practically all the furnishings here of wood and fabric, reproducible with the same technology used for those human beings and animals buried in the ash layer. Voids in the ash soil generated by organic materials that have long decomposed but left an imprint, a 'negative' in the ground, are filled with plaster to salvage the form of decomposed organic materials (wood, leather, fabric etc.).

There they stood before us, each against one wall: two beds 1.7 metres long and one smaller one, apparently for a child. The label 'bed' is a slight exaggeration: round horizontal poles are stuck into four angular corner posts; the whole thing can be taken apart and reassembled in five minutes. When the child gets bigger, you simply replace the lengthwise poles; to turn a single bed into a double you just have to substitute the crosswise poles with longer ones.

Mattresses? You must be joking: there weren't any. Nor did these beds have any slats. Ropes and cords were fixed to the horizontal poles – the imprints of these have been preserved in the solidified ash – to form a sort of hammock or, more accurately, a net. A woollen blanket on top and it was done. Imprints of these woollen blankets have also been preserved. They show that on that autumn day in 79 CE there was no time to make the beds. The blankets lay scrunched up on top.

Apart from a chamber pot under each bed there was also a simple clay jug, probably for water. Amphorae were found lying here too, unsealed. Unfortunately they were partly destroyed by the tunnels of the grave robbers working along the lengths of the walls, as were the sides of the beds against these walls. We suspect that the amphorae under the beds were the 'suitcases' of the slaves living here, where they kept items of clothing or other personal effects.

This new and unique evidence gives us a glimpse into three lives, each squashed into 5 square metres where they slept, drank and went to the lavatory – and worked too. The room wasn't 'only' for living in, it also served as a work and storage space. Leaning in the corners were amphorae for wine, oil or grain (their contents are currently being analysed).

In the middle of the room was a small wooden box, likewise preserved by the hot ash, containing bridles. It seems that, when disaster struck, they were in the process of harnessing the carriage that was right outside the door to the room. This is confirmed by a particular find that caused us a real headache at first, because to our knowledge no similar object had ever been excavated from an ancient Roman settlement. Only when we made comparisons with modern horse carts did the solution materialise. What we had was the plaster cast of an ancient carriage shaft, consisting of wood, ropes, leather and iron, leaning against one of the beds where it was still standing despite the hasty flight and ash storm.

Opposite the door, high up in the wall, was a tiny window. Beneath it a rectangle of white plaster, the only decoration – if we can even call it that – of the otherwise unrendered wall. In the middle of that rectangle was a nail. Our assumption that it was for hanging an oil lamp was confirmed by the excavation. We did indeed find a clay lamp by the wall, smashed on the floor at the moment of the eruption. The white patch on the wall was there to reflect the weak light from the lamp, thereby slightly amplifying it.

This rectangle had been visible prior to the recent excavation of the last metre of ash layers covering the furniture, but ever since I understood the history behind it, i.e. the rest of the room, I've found it very moving. It certainly wouldn't have been the villa's owner who'd thought about this minimal improvement in comfort: optimising the dim lighting. The people living in the room must have done it themselves. But how, if you were a slave and couldn't just call on the painter? I imagine someone living here perhaps going to the painters and plasterers working in the grand part of the villa, begging and begging until the master craftsman sent his apprentice to plaster this nuisance's white rectangle on the wall, for Hercules's sake. Or maybe a friendship had developed and the patch of white was a small present, perhaps unsolicited, given by the painter's apprentice to the young slave girl who slept here and in the evenings liked to play with dolls and dice in the light of the lamp.

A CITY ON THE VERGE OF CATASTROPHE

As well as making an impression on my team and me, the discovery of the slave quarters in November 2021 also resonated with the Italian and international press. How did this happen? Or, to put it differently, how do archaeologists communicate their discoveries to the media? There are two extreme views on this, both wrong. One borders on naïvety, the other belongs to the realm of conspiracy theories.

The naïve view says that we archaeologists simply pass on information about everything we find and then it's up to journalists to determine what's worth a headline on the front page. It doesn't work that way, of course. In general journalists are well educated, informed and extremely receptive, but they can't be experts in every field. Therefore if you run an archaeological park like Pompeii, you have to develop a sense of what you can communicate to the media and how. This is anything but a secondary skill, because it lies at the very heart of the issue of how archaeology communicates with society.

When I started work in Paestum in 2015 I was fortunate to have a guardian angel. One day Patrizia Nicoletti came to my office, offering her assistance. In 1980 she'd started working as an art historian in the Ministry of Culture, after the severe earthquake that had hit the region of Campania, killing more than 3,000 people. Her first few years in heritage conservation were spent inspecting churches, monasteries, palazzi and other cultural assets that had either fallen down or were at risk of collapse. Alongside her work she'd trained to become a communications specialist and now she was getting slightly bored in heritage conservation. Well, she didn't need to feel bored any longer because she played a key role in the adventure of turning

Paestum into a modern, independent park in the final years before her retirement.

From her I learned that although communication isn't everything, everything is communication. This means that communication doesn't begin with the press release and end with social media. Communication starts inside the organisation, specifically with how we talk to each other on a daily basis. If you look closely, it's easy to see that around 80 per cent of archaeology and museum work is communication – in management you can confidently assume that this figure is 90 per cent. A director is like a conductor who doesn't play a note themselves, but ensures that sixty musicians play together in harmony. It's all down to the communication.

I talked through all the texts with Patrizia, all the press releases as well as articles I wrote for daily papers, interviews, important letters and even instructions to staff that had the potential to stir discontent. With her calm, always slightly smoky voice she never tired of airing her concerns and suggestions for improvement, all done with brutal honesty.

Paestum was difficult, especially at the beginning. We had to conjure everything out of nothing, from the press office to the accounts department. On the other hand this was what made the enterprise easy; if you start from nothing, you've got plenty of space in which to grow. Every small step of progress was gratefully received.

Pompeii is a completely different story. There are almost ten times the number of visitors. And the communication follows a very different logic. We are in the eye of the hurricane. Whereas in Paestum I would scroll through the press reviews in the hope

A CITY ON THE VERGE OF CATASTROPHE

of finding our park mentioned in the important national papers, in Pompeii I'm delighted if there's nothing in the papers about us except for on those days when we put out a press release. Writing about real or supposed scandals, accidents, problems and intrigues in Pompeii seems to increase circulation. At any rate the press goes crazy for them, especially the minor papers sadly fighting for survival and clutching at every straw.

Here's one example. A few months after I took up my post in Pompeii the local police discovered an illegal cannabis plantation on a former industrial site that the park was converting for use into an exhibition space and museum depot. The local press turned this into: 'Cannabis plantation discovered in Pompeii', 'Cannabis plantation in archaeological park', 'Cannabis planted in Pompeii excavations' etc. Of course, readers wondered how something like this could possibly happen in a World Heritage Site. And yet the industrial site isn't even in the modern municipality of Pompeii, but in the neighbouring one, Scafati.

Marella Brunetto, head of the Pompeii press office, isn't fazed by this sort of thing. She's been through worse. She was responsible for communication when walls in Pompeii used to collapse on a monthly basis even though there was money in the park's account, because the management wasn't capable of getting the restoration projects under way. Afterwards, from a professional point of view, she went from the very bottom to the top on the wheel of fortune. When, thanks to a large-scale EU-funded project, Pompeii finally made positive headlines around the world again, Marella breathed a sigh of relief even though her work increased rather than decreased.

THE BURIED CITY

In terms of visibility, Pompeii is vertiginously high up. A mountain can be made of every molehill. With Marella as co-pilot we try to circumnavigate air pockets and turbulence. When an important find is made we ensure that no photographs or details leak out before the official announcement, so we don't lose control. We also try to avoid, insofar as this is predictable, going public on days when other events of national importance are on the agenda. And of course, everything is planned so that we can accede to requests for television interviews on site. This means that I'm not on a work trip 'the day after' or scheduled to be elsewhere.

But that's about it. One day here, one day there . . . allow the excavation to continue a while longer or make an announcement about interim findings – that's the leeway we have. Obviously we're thrilled by every new discovery. And I confess, there's a touch of pride in what we do too. Archaeology is teamwork that demands a lot of patience and hard work from all involved. A pleasing discovery is an oasis where the caravan rests before undertaking the next barren spell. And yes, it's also true that an archaeological park that becomes a talking point through new research and discoveries will attract the public. But all these are byproducts, welcome but not crucial. The real reason we foster this form of communication is a different one. Archaeology and heritage conservation are financed by society, whether through entrance tickets, taxes or donations. In return I believe we have a duty to keep the public informed about the findings of our work. This ought to be done promptly and in a way that's intelligible to everyone, rather than just in specialist publications that nobody outside of the discipline understands, and which take years or even decades to appear.

A CITY ON THE VERGE OF CATASTROPHE

Sadly, a small but vociferous section of the Italian public sees this differently. Their reproach aimed at directors who communicate proactively is that this amounts to sensationalism. They believe it's *scoperte a orologeria*, which translates roughly as 'discoveries by the clock'. As if we had a secret plan providing for a 'sensational discovery' every few months that we pull out of a hat – maybe even on instructions from the highest echelons in the ministry, subtly using the archaeological sensations to distract from other matters, and always at precisely the right moment!

Anyone familiar with the craft of excavation knows how absurd this idea is. But, like every conspiracy theory, this one too is immune to all objective argument. On the contrary, any evidence of the innocence of our actions is seen as further proof of our cunning that leads others astray. Surely there must be some devilish plan behind this. The more you get bogged down in such speculation, the more difficult it becomes – I imagine – to admit that actually the whole thing is quite simple: who digs finds. And who finds ought to be accountable to the citizens financing the search, shouldn't they?

When we unveiled the slave quarters in Civita Giuliana, *Il Fatto Quotidiano*, one of Italy's most important daily papers, ran the headline: 'Pompeii & Company: Hyped-Up Scoops Amid Millions of Indiscriminate Funding and Personal Careers'.[38] The whole thing, the paper claimed, was nothing but a torrent of plaster poured into cavities in the floor (which from a purely technical point of view was correct), and once again was being sold as a 'sensational discovery' for 'marketing' and 'propaganda' purposes.

I rang the editor-in-chief and asked to be given the chance to respond. My text was published in full, albeit with a different title from the one I'd suggested. This almost always happens, even to in-house journalists. The headlines are written by the editors who are responsible for how the page looks overall.

I was lucky because the title they chose was better than mine: '"Slave Room" in Pompeii: The Rarity of the Everyday'. This really nailed the distinctiveness of the discovery. But the 'rarity of the everyday' could also be the title for my personal access to archaeology and Pompeii. The fuel for my engine, so to speak.

We ought to bear in mind that history-writing and archaeology produce a distorted picture of the world, one that is upside down, as it were. Texts, inscriptions, buildings, graves, which are created by a tiny minority of rich and powerful people, constitute the overwhelming majority of our sources. What has scarcity value in our present day – the world of the super-rich and powerful – thus dominates our view of the ancient Roman world.

To a certain extent this is in the nature of how material is handed down. The poor seldom write diaries, letters and discourses, and these are preserved even more rarely. The conditions of archaeological preservation favour the ancient upper class too: temples, palaces and mausoleums leave behind more durable traces than huts, tents and workshops. And so the perspective of the elite veils the reality of ancient life like a screen onto which a very particular vision of reality is projected. For example, what we know about the lives of slaves in antiquity comes almost exclusively from texts written by slaveowners or inscriptions from a small group of freedmen who became rich.

A CITY ON THE VERGE OF CATASTROPHE

And more than 90 per cent of what we know about the lives of women in antiquity comes from the pens of men.

Pompeii is like a rip in the screen, through which we have the opportunity to take a peek behind the official version of history. What's special about Pompeii, therefore, aren't its temples (the temples of Paestum and Pozzuoli are much more stupendous) or the amphitheatre or theatre (larger ones can be found in Rome, Capua or Verona). It's far more the fabric of workshops, apartments, taverns, boarding houses, shops, baths and bordellos that make Pompeii a unique place for archaeology. Even the city's famous wall paintings are less valuable for their artistic merit (even though some are not far off the quality of the frescoes from the imperial palaces in Rome) than for their number and preservation in situ. This makes it possible to understand ancient art in its environment, as part of everyday life in the houses of the upper and middle classes.

The slave room in Civita Giuliana opens the tear in the screen a bit further. So this is how slaves lived, people who only ever appear marginally in the texts of ancient writers and about whose bedrooms barely a word has been written. Or does the room also open up a window onto the daily life of legally free women and men who lived in poor circumstances? Was what we see here – three beds in a confined space – actually the everyday reality of the majority of Pompeii's population?

I think the answer is yes. But to explain this, we need to go a bit further afield to another discovery from 2022 that appears to confirm the hypothesis. We can only say this much: in the last decades before the eruption of Vesuvius in 79 CE Pompeii was living on the threshold of disaster, not just because of the looming eruption, but because the city was economically and socially on shaky ground, ever on the verge of collapse.

To get an idea of life in ancient Pompeii it's important to know how many people lived in the city. It makes a difference whether on average a room houses one or three people, even if we're only talking about mean values that at best allow us to approximate the reality of everyday life in antiquity.

My grandparents' generation could have said a thing or two about this. After the Second World War, when much housing was destroyed (including my mother's parents' home in Regensburg), people who were bombed out and refugees from East Prussia were billeted wherever possible. The houses and flats were the same, but life in cramped conditions – often sharing with total strangers – changed radically.

After a few years they moved to one of the blocks of flats that were conjured out of nothing on the edge of Regensburg. My mother slept in a tiny room on a foldaway bed that my sister and I used as children when we had visitors. Until my mother's two brothers moved out they slept in the sitting room, which every evening was transformed from a sterile reception room into a sleeping area, and put back again every morning before school. This was all on account of the hypothetical possibility that somebody might turn up unannounced who would then need to be given coffee and biscuits in the sitting room. As this occurred very seldom the room remained virtually unused during the day. The only cosy room (and the only one properly heated in winter) was the kitchen, because this was the realm of my grandmother, who was the emotional central heating of the family too. The kitchen bench could be flipped up and used as a chest, while it also served as an additional bed.

One of my colleagues in Paestum slept on a very similar bench as a child in a small inland village, on the slopes of the Alburni mountains. From Roscigno (as the village is called) you can see the sea, but the peasants who went into the fields with their donkeys until the 1970s had never swum in it. They would have found the very idea absurd, like someone suggesting they take a walk on the moon. Domenico's family of four lived in two rooms, one of which was the kitchen. By today's standards that's a one-bedroom flat, and this was already progress, for when Domenico was born in 1960 the family still lived in a single room that contained everything – and had no door! As it was partitioned off from a flat and didn't have its own entrance you had to climb in and out of the window.

Prone to the risk of severe landslides, the entire village was relocated at the beginning of the twentieth century. The old village, Roscigno Vecchio, a sort of nineteenth-century Pompeii, is decaying, less than two kilometres from the new one. The local heritage association offers tours. Apart from how cramped the place is, I've always been struck by the scale of the houses and furniture. It's as if everything is a few sizes smaller, thus creating the same impression of dolls' houses that Goethe described in Pompeii. From the fork to the chair, table and chest, everything is smaller than you would usually find today.

THE BURIED CITY

To me everything seems more beautiful, human, modest. I'd happily spend a night in a kitchen in Roscigno Vecchio: wood stove, tiny table, chairs that look as if they're for children, small plates and tin forks. Our stainless-steel cutlery appears oversized by comparison, our chairs like ludicrous thrones of an overweight consumer society, our sofas like material guarantees that we won't inadvertently get too close to each other when watching television.

Today Roscigno is suffering from the depopulation that first hit the mountainous interior of Campania in the 1990s and has since grown to a dramatic scale. Where 2,000 people once lived, only 640 inhabitants are now registered. Many of them actually live elsewhere for professional reasons. Young people in particular are moving away; fields and olive groves are becoming overgrown. In the multistorey house where Domenico's family used to live in one room on the ground floor, a single old man resides on his own.

If this house were to be excavated by archaeologists in a thousand years, what would remain of its history? The same house, which was once home to about thirty people and is now as good as empty – what traces of its story would survive in the ground?

This describes quite well the problem we have in Pompeii. Although we know about two-thirds of the ancient city and have an incomparably precise idea of the residential quarter, estimates as to how many people lived here diverge wildly. It's no coincidence, perhaps, that earlier generations of archaeologists, who themselves experienced a cramped world of smallness, assumed a substantially denser population than archaeologists of the post-war period and recent past.

A CITY ON THE VERGE OF CATASTROPHE

In the second half of the nineteenth century Giuseppe Fiorelli, who was the first to make plaster casts of the victims of Vesuvius, reckoned on a population of 12,000 people. Others found his figure too low. Heinrich Nissen, a German ancient historian, estimated 20,000 inhabitants. His countryman Karl Julius Beloch, who at the age of sixteen emigrated to Sorrento near Pompeii because he was suffering from tuberculosis, and became a professor in Italy, was more circumspect. He estimated the population of the ancient city to have been 15,000.

More recent calculations from the post-war era to recent times have gone even lower than Fiorelli. They range from 8,000 to a maximum of 12,000 inhabitants. How this affects our picture of life in ancient Pompeii can be seen in a 1975 article written by an American archaeologist. In 'Middle and lower class housing in Pompeii and Herculaneum' James Packer comes to the conclusion that the 'lower classes' in Pompeii lived in 'surprising comfort', enjoying a standard of living 'not equalled again in western Europe until the nineteenth century after Christ'. He bases this assessment on the extensive living space he believed was available.[39]

But then something happened, something that makes archaeology so unpredictable and fascinating. A discovery that nobody was looking for, let alone expecting, and which forces us after 150 years to thoroughly question what appeared to be progress.

It is 2017 and construction work begins on the 'San Paolino' office complex, outside the Stabian Gate on the road paved with large basalt stones, which in antiquity connected Pompeii with Stabiae. The two-storey, nineteenth-century building is going to be converted into a library with guest rooms for researchers from around the world. To accomplish this the terrain sloping down steeply towards the road needs to be flattened. It's possible that remains of ancient graves that usually lined the arterial roads will be uncovered. This was because it was forbidden for religious reasons to bury the dead within the city walls. As in all ancient cities, the monuments to the dead were the first thing people saw when they arrived – and the last when they left the city.

The discovery of the grave outside the Stabian Gate, which belonged to one of the most influential men of the city's final years, was a surprise, however. The funerary monument has a peculiar form: a rectangle with concave walls. But the most interesting thing about the tomb is the fact that it's emblazoned with the longest grave inscription ever found in Pompeii. The text recalls the life's work of the tomb's owner, who may have still been alive at the time of the eruption and had merely had it prepared in advance (which happened frequently).[40]

For ancient Romans this chiefly involved listing the offices they had held and philanthropic things they'd done for the community. The latter was essential for anyone keen on a successful career. Ancient politicians and dignitaries weren't paid; on the contrary, they were expected to finance building works, gladiatorial games, circus races, theatrical productions and the like. For this they had to dig deep into their pockets. What at first may appear as exemplary to many people disenchanted with politics, who moan about their politicians' benefits and salaries, turns out on closer inspection to be a deeply undemocratic feature of Roman politics. Only the rich were able to take part in the political discussion.

Not only did nepotism and clientship flourish, they were officially recognised as part of the political system. Citizens from the lower and middle classes entrusted themselves as 'clients' to a *patronus*, a rich citizen with political ambitions who would bail them out when necessary. This could be a small loan with favourable conditions, a recommendation or useful contacts when there were difficulties with the authorities. In return the *patronus* could count on the votes of his clients when applying for an office. Freed slaves were also expected to remain bonded to their former masters as clients, even if they later surpassed them in wealth.

Without an awareness of this social system we cannot properly begin to understand the structure of the Roman house. In the centre was the atrium, a courtyard-like area that led to bedrooms and work rooms. The roof was open in the middle so rainwater could collect in the impluvium for the internal cisterns.

The entrance to the house led directly into the atrium; opposite was the tablinum where every morning the master of the house received clients, petitioners and business partners. They would wait in the atrium, and the manner in which a person waited reflected their social status. The more comfortable and closer to the tablinum you were, the higher the master of the house held you in regard and favour. His social status was reflected in the atrium too and not only in its architecture. The more people sitting in the atrium, the 'waiting room' of the family business, the more important its owner must be. If he travelled to Rome for political or financial reasons, it might well be the case that he himself would be a petitioner waiting in the atrium of a senator.

Some houses in Pompeii have waiting rooms that continue onto the street, as it were: benches outside the house where clients and petitioners would wait. Whenever you see such benches in Pompeii, for example outside the House of the Ceii, you can assume that an important man lived here – or was it just one who was bluffing? To be sure, you would have to know how many people actually waited on those benches every morning and what business had brought them here.

Which brings us back to the question of how many people there were. How many people lived in Pompeii, how many petitioners did a person have to help to become a somebody in the city or even to secure one of the city's political offices?

The answer suggested by the grave outside the Stabian Gate amounts to far higher than the boldest estimates. The inscription begins with the party that the tomb owner threw for the people when he was awarded the *toga virilis*, the male toga that marked a man's entry into adulthood:

HIC TOGAE VIRILIS SUAE EPULUM POPULO POMPEIANO TRICLINIS CCCCLVI ITA UT IN TRICLINIS QUINIDENI HOMINES DISCUMBERENT . . . DEDIT

On receiving his male toga this man held a celebratory dinner for the people of Pompeii, consisting of 456 tricliniums with fifteen men at each triclinium . . .

Fired-clay statue from the sanctuary of Fondo Iozzino outside the gates of Pompeii at the mouth of the River Sarno.

View of the atrium of the Villa of the Mysteries with in situ casts of the victims of the eruption.

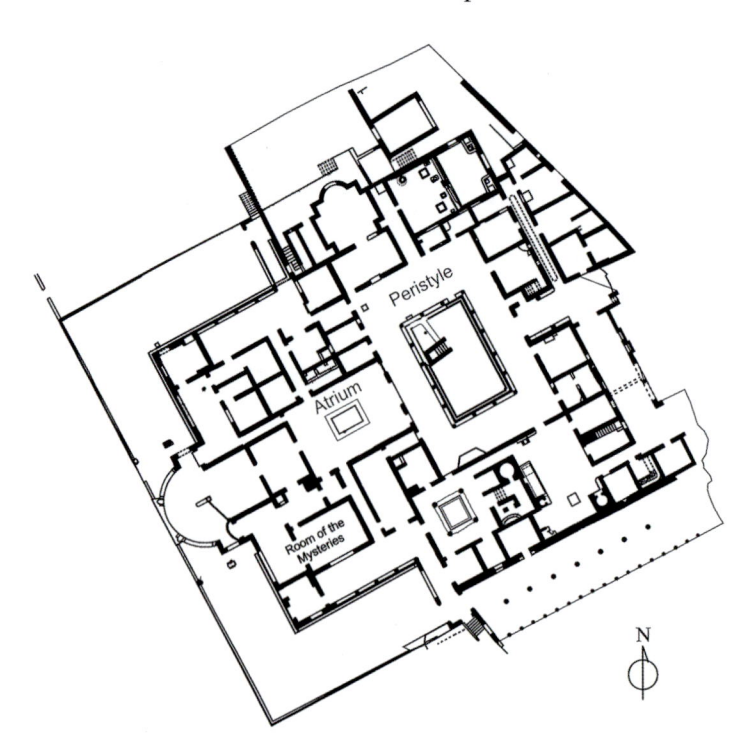

Plan of the Villa of the Mysteries. The room known as the 'Room of the Mysteries' houses the frieze from which the villa gets its name.

The frieze probably begins in the north-west corner. A woman is sitting on a
richly decorated chair; on the armrest to the right is a writing tablet –
her daughter's marriage contract?

Room for secret mysteries or decorated living room?
View of the north and east walls.

Detail from the north wall: women performing rituals; a boy reading from a scroll.

In the middle of the east wall a couple: Dionysus and Ariadne (or Semele?). To the right a woman crouching beside a hidden object; next to her a winged figure preparing to use a whip.

Detail from the north wall: sileni and pointy-eared wood spirits making music. One of them is breastfeeding a kid goat.

On the south wall the flagellation scene from the east wall continues.
Beside this is a dancing woman with cymbals.

The frieze ends with a young woman, presumably a bride at her toilette, surrounded by two winged Cupids.

The ceremonial chariot from the villa at Civita Giuliana.

The chariot was buried almost completely by volcanic ash.

Silver-plated medallions with erotic motifs on the back of the chariot.

The 'slave room' in the villa at Civita Giuliana.

The lararium (house altar) in a house in Pompeii excavated in 2018, which has been given the name House of the Lararium.

A cupboard with crockery and supplies that came to light in the course of recent excavations in the House of the Lararium in 2022.

Excavation of a room with pallet bed, opened chest, small table and 'kitchenette' in the House of the Lararium, summer 2022.

At the rear of the House of the Lararium the excavations uncovered a room with two beds.

The front of the grave of Marcus Venerius Secundio outside the Sarno Gate.
The blue base colour of the painting suggests that most of the
plants depicted there have faded.

First glimpse inside the just-opened grave chamber of M. Venerius Secundio.
After this speed was of the essence.

Plaster cast of a gate with integrated night door on Via del'Abbondanza.

Entrance to a typical basso in Naples. To the left a small altar, similar to the ones found in the streets of ancient Pompeii.

A group of victims of the volcanic eruption from the House of the Golden Bracelet, kept in Pompeii's Antiquarium.

Sheep helping to mow the grass in the archaeological park, December 2022.

The 'pizza' fresco: a still life of pita-like bread with fruits (dates, pomegranates) and spices that resembles a modern-day pizza, on the wall of the hall, or atrium, of a house in Regio IX.

Fresco depicting Helen of Troy meeting Paris on the north wall of the 'black dining room', next door to the 'pizza' fresco. The walls of the room were painted black to disguise the smoke of the oil lamps when guests gathered here for lavish banquets.

Apollo and Cassandra on the south wall of the black dining room. The paintings date to the third style, which means that they were already several decades old when Mount Vesuvius erupted.

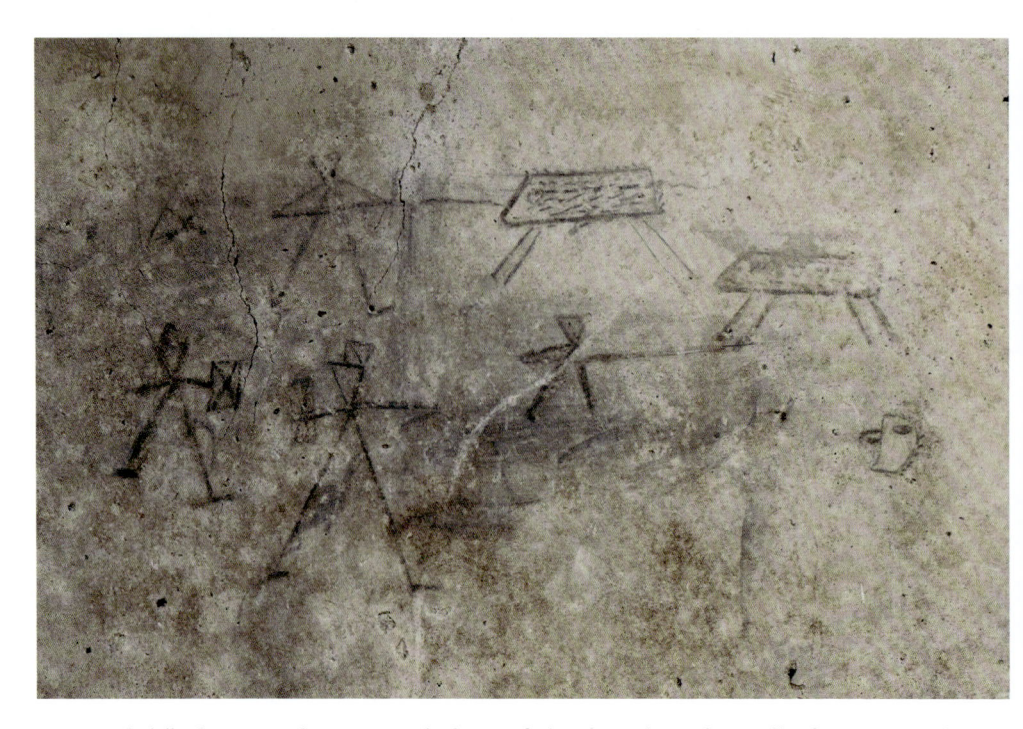

A child's drawing showing a gladiator fight, found on the wall of a courtyard. A nearby handprint indicates the child was around seven years old.

A CITY ON THE VERGE OF CATASTROPHE

In antiquity the expression 'people of Pompeii' – *populus Pompeianus* – had a relatively specific meaning. It's not for nothing that the phrase 'Roman people' – *populus Romanus* – appears in the official expression *Senatus Populusque Romanus* ('The Senate and the Roman people', shortened to *SPQR*) that still adorns the cast-iron manhole covers of the Italian capital. The word *populus*, from which the English word 'popular' comes (as well as its shortened form 'pop'), originally meant the enfranchised male citizens of a city state. For 'people' in the sense of the common folk, the 'riff-raff', they used the word *plebs* in antiquity. The *plebs* also included non-citizens, women and children, in short all the 'filler material' (*plebs* comes from *complere*, 'to fill, fill up') that from the perspective of the male citizens was necessary to keep the state going without actually being involved in the running of it.

We can easily calculate how many citizens there were: 456 tricliniums of fifteen men each makes 6,840. That's how many male citizens lived in ancient Pompeii at the time when the tomb owner came of age, which must have been before the middle of the first century CE, as we can conclude from other passages in the inscription. The man's name hasn't been recorded for posterity, but Massimo Osanna showed that in all likelihood he was Gnaeus Alleius Nigidius Maius, probably the most influential politician in Pompeii in the decades leading up to the eruption of Mount Vesuvius.

Given almost 7,000 male citizens it's clear that estimates of 8,000 inhabitants are pretty wide of the mark. To the number of male citizens we have to add women, children, non-citizens, slaves and people with a second residence in Pompeii who might have only been there sporadically, but maintained a household including servants and a manager with family. Together with the historian Elio Lo Cascio, Osanna estimates a total population of up to 45,000 people, including slaves.[41]

Such a figure – 45,000 people – is twice as many as the most ambitious estimates in 150 years of scholarly discussions, and four to five times as many as was commonly assumed by scholars until recently. This drastically transforms our image of the ancient city. Broken down to the family level this is equivalent to a home that suddenly has to have space for fourteen people rather than four. Which is a change on the scale that my grandparents experienced at the end of the war. The difference is that the shift in numbers for ancient Pompeii is not a consequence of war and expulsion, but of the imponderables of modern research. A single chance discovery can shake decades-old certainties.

The question is: where did all these people find space? How 'small and cramped', to use Goethe's words, was Pompeii in fact, if so many people lived in the city?

A computer can help us find an answer. The use of digital technology in the humanities is particularly important in archaeology, where we are dealing with large amounts of hard-to-grasp data that doesn't speak to us as directly as a historical textual source. Pompeii is a good example here.

A CITY ON THE VERGE OF CATASTROPHE

If you wish to accommodate five people in a flat, this is probably best done by looking at the rooms. If you want to house five families in a block of flats, a plan of the building is certainly useful. But what if you have to distribute tens of thousands of people across an entire city (even if just from the archaeologist's desk)? A city, moreover, that first was submerged by Vesuvius and lay dormant beneath the earth for centuries, and second is far from having been fully excavated. Around a third of the ancient city is still underground.

In such cases a GIS, or Geographic Information System, is of great help. Being able to link an almost unlimited number of tables and data with digital maps allows us to play out various scenarios and models. We can also draft hypotheses for the as yet unexcavated area of the city. Technically we speak of 'extrapolating': projecting data from a known area onto an unknown one. Although we don't know exactly what's lying underground, we can establish a rough estimate – this in a nutshell is the logic behind it.

We've had our own GIS in Pompeii for several years, parts of which have also been available to external users since 2022 via the 'Open Pompeii' website (open.pompeiisites.org). With its help we can organise the buildings in the ancient city into all possible categories, including function. Is this a temple, a workshop or a home? Of course, we can argue over individual cases, such as when a workshop might also have served as somewhere to live. But we can assume that the number of residential buildings is roughly correct.

I'm aware that the number of 'roughly correct' claims in this chapter is getting ever bigger: number of inhabitants, number of non-excavated houses, number of homes . . . This is unavoidable, unfortunately, and incidentally one of the main problems facing everyone researching ancient social history. The primary sources are simply miserable. Historians of more recent periods used to dealing with archival data such as tax lists or baptism registers can only shake their heads in disbelief when they see how we piece together the social history of ancient city states such as Pompeii, Rome or Athens from scattered (and often contradictory) written sources and archaeological speculation. But research sometimes means asking questions without the prospect of clear answers. A good question frequently leads to further progress in research than supposedly 'fail-safe' answers do.

If our GIS database is to be believed, the excavated section of Pompeii comprises 1,076 residential units. These range from one-room dwellings that also served as shops to the House of the Faun with more than fifty rooms on the ground floor (there were dozens more on the first floor that has not survived). If we extrapolate this figure onto the non-excavated part of the city, we arrive at around 1,400 dwellings in ancient Pompeii.

But before we apportion the (assumed) number of inhabitants to the (assumed) number of residential units we have to clarify one thing: a section of the population must have lived in the countryside. Many villas and farms have been excavated in the area surrounding Pompeii. Oplontis on the coast even extended to the size of a small settlement with a few hundred inhabitants.

All the same, I think that the percentage of those who lived in the countryside was far lower than is commonly assumed. It has been widely held that the proportion of the total population living in urban areas in the Roman Empire was between 15 and 20 per cent. Particularly bold estimates put this figure between 25 and 30 per cent. According to such assumptions, the majority of the 45,000 people who lived in Pompeii would have been rural dwellers. But there's nothing in the ancient sources to corroborate such an assumption. I suspect rather that the low estimates – often unconsciously, for sure – are influenced by the paradigm of historical evolutionism.

The term 'historical evolutionism' refers to a particular view of the history of humanity that proliferated in the eighteenth and nineteenth centuries in Europe. In this period European states colonised other parts of the globe, plundering their resources and cultural goods, subduing, enslaving and mistreating their peoples. But the horror was suppressed in the public consciousness, and colonialism was presented as a civilising act. Europe saw itself as a pioneer in science, culture and religion – researchers and missionaries followed in the footsteps of the conquerors. They saw themselves at the apex of progress in civilisation. European scholars believed they could find older stages of their own culture in the 'primitive' peoples of other continents, as if all cultures went through the same stages of development but some were simply more advanced than others.

Central to this history of development (or 'evolution'),

however, was another idea: that there is continual progress upwards. The more advanced and civilised a culture, the higher it ranks. 'Better' – in the sense of 'superior' – than the Stone Age is the Bronze Age, and even 'better' is the Iron Age. Right at the top – from the European perspective – stood the Europeans themselves.

If you look closely, you can still find traces of this way of thinking, even though it isn't promoted as openly as it was at the height of colonialism. For example, we occasionally hear talk of 'Stone Age communism' or a return to the 'dark' Middle Ages to criticise certain phenomena or regimes of our own time. Behind this, quite apart from whether the implicit criticism is correct, is a disparaging view of the Stone Age or the Middle Ages.

We tend to feel superior to the people from these periods because we fly in aeroplanes or own smartphones. In truth the people of the Stone Age possessed skills and knowledge that we have long forgotten. And without the Middle Ages we would have virtually nothing from the ancient philosophers and writers, for most of it was preserved only thanks to mediaeval manuscripts.

What does all of this have to do with the relationship between the urban and rural populations in the Roman Empire? The point is, the notion of history running along certain lines of development has been applied to Europe's own past too.

From the perspective of evolutionary history the line goes from village to town and from there to the megacity of the future. This is directly reflected in our experience of the present and expectations for the future, which governments, experts and organisations like the United Nations persuade us into thinking. For example, a 2018 article by Hannah Ritchie and Max Roser said: 'More than half of the world's population now live in urban areas – increasingly in highly-dense cities. However, urban settings are a relatively new phenomenon in human history. This transition has transformed the way we live, work, travel and build networks.'[42]

I am not denying that the megacities of our time represent something new. What's problematic about the text quoted above, however, is that it's written into a historical one-way street that leads from pre-modern and pre-industrial societies (= village) to the modern (= city).

Such examples of evolutionist approaches to history don't only narrow our view of the future, which appears preordained to go down the same one-way street (but why, in fact?), they also condition our view of the past. Anybody who has taken this on board will find it hard to imagine that in antiquity a higher percentage of people lived in cities than, let's say, in Germany or Britain at the start of the Industrial Revolution. For this would violate the traffic regulations of evolutionary historical science: going the wrong way down a one-way street!

This is not to say that colleagues who estimate the proportion of people living in cities in antiquity to be very low adhere to evolutionist or even colonialist ideologies. All of us in this field are part of an intergenerational dialogue, a large river with tributaries and crosscurrents, the depths and branches of which are only partly clear. The beam in one's own eye is always the hardest thing to see.

THE BURIED CITY

The mindset in history and archaeology towards the topics of 'development' and 'progress' must also subconsciously be connected to our experience of the present. For example, I've always instinctively resisted the idea that I'm somehow more advanced than previous generations. Maybe because I belong to a generation that from childhood was confronted with the terrors of nuclear annihilation and environmental destruction. Along with my sister I took part in my first demonstration against nuclear power when I was still in my pram, and a photo of this appeared in the local paper. The Chernobyl nuclear disaster, on 26 April 1986, is one of the few days from my pre-school years that I can remember. We were playing out in the courtyard when my mother appeared and said we had to come in. We moaned but she was insistent and we could sense her distress.

Today, now that the man-made climate change we've been warned about for decades has come to pass, we might doubt more than ever humanity's capacity for progress. At any rate arrogance towards earlier eras is inappropriate, not least because the much-feted achievements in prosperity, modern medicine etc. only benefit a minority from a global perspective.

Such unease towards the present day naturally sharpens our perception of real or supposed incongruities in the reconstruction of the past. Those who optimistically believe that everything is pretty much fantastic these days are perhaps less receptive to this. We could also say less prejudiced. For a fundamentally critical view of the present harbours dangers too, the greatest of which is only ever looking back at the past for what is good. This is merely turning the narrative of progress on its head, which is just as questionable. It leads to the search for an original equilibrium, a better existence from which we humans at some point strayed because of some fatal development. For some people that tipping point is industrialisation (from 1800), for others the Enlightenment, colonialism, racism, the modern era (let's say from the French Revolution, which perhaps wasn't such a brilliant development after all – remember the guillotine?). Or did the downfall begin much earlier? With the invention of money (around 600 BCE) . . . of writing (around 3000 BCE) . . . of agriculture, that's to say in the Neolithic Age (around 9000 BCE)? Perhaps the last time we were fulfilled, free people was when we lived nomadic lives, struggling along as hunters and gatherers? Is the cave art that survives from an infinitely distant world not just the first but also the greatest art, never to be equalled again and compared to which Pompeii's paintings, even the much-vaunted Greek classicism, are only a faint coda?

In Thomas Mann's *Doctor Faustus* such fantasies are played out using music. In this novel the conversations between the characters about the decline in 'true' music float to ever more absurd heights. At some point even Monteverdi and Bach appear as decadent latecomers.

I have to admit that when I read the book I recognised parts of myself, not because of Monteverdi or Bach, both of whom I adore. But my fascination for antiquity is probably also driven by a similar romantic desire to find not only a different world in the past, but one that was more genuine, truer and better.

This is part of my engine, as I've become aware over time. It drifts in this direction. I know it and make efforts to steer against it to avoid deviating from the road of objective argumentation. I'm an archaeologist with a bias. But ultimately so are we all, because there is no straight road back to the past. The past isn't a rational 'destination'; it can't be. And at least I'm aware of my bias.

What, then, if Pompeii wasn't a neat little town with a village-like tranquillity, from which it would take many centuries to arrive at the congested metropolises of the looming industrial age? What if in Pompeii the sustainability problem of the modern city had already to some extent become reality? What if we're not looking at a stable, agricultural entity but a seething, crowded agglomeration, permanently on the verge of some social catastrophe?

This is indeed the impression we get as a result of analysing the distribution of farms and villas surrounding Pompeii, as well as inscriptions relating to the population of the city's territory. For it seems unlikely that more than 50 per cent of citizens along with their families and slaves, insofar as they had them, had their main domicile in the countryside. Of the 45,000 people who lived in Pompeii according to the inscription at the Stabian Gate, at least 20,000 must have resided in the city itself. Probably the figure was even higher.

Correspondingly the living space inside the city was cramped. Each of the approximately 1,400 dwellings that existed according to our GIS-based estimate was home to two or three male citizens. On top of this there were the women, children and slaves. That makes an average of fourteen people per dwelling. These could consist of just one or two rooms at floor level, which was true of almost two-thirds of all homes in Pompeii, around 900.[43]

It's more difficult to say how many people on average lived in a room. For one thing, not all rooms served as living rooms or bedrooms, even though given the circumstances described we must suppose that members of the lower class, be they slaves or free individuals, often slept in work rooms and corridors. Also, almost all of the upper floors are missing because in most cases they fell victim to the pyroclastic blast waves. Whatever stood above the 3-metre-high lapilli layers was swept away.

We can only calculate very roughly how the population was distributed among the existing rooms, well aware that not all rooms were slept in and that there were more rooms than recorded by our GIS. With the numbers to hand we arrive at about two people per room, an astonishingly high figure. Even if, as we've said, the numbers are only approximate, Pompeii was a city bursting with people.

If you look closely, you can find clues to this everywhere. Inscriptions advertise top-floor homes for rent. Building conversions too are testimony to the attempt to make use of every available square metre. Rooms and shops are divided off from the house, with separate entrances and outdoor staircases. This can only have been done for rental purposes.

When excavating the House of the Lararium in 2022, we discovered a room that perfectly illustrates Goethe's description of 'small and cramped'. Behind a courtyard with a beautifully painted family altar (lararium), which also housed a kitchen and, below the wooden stairs, a latrine, are five simple rooms on two floors. The floors are of tamped earth mixed with some marl – a naturally found blend of clay and calcium carbonate – and no paintings adorn the walls. The smart area of the house is probably in the part of the city still to be excavated.

In one of the rooms we were able to reclaim almost all the furniture as plaster casts. The 9-square-metre space was pretty crammed. In one corner stood a bed, big enough to fit two people if necessary. What's interesting is that it has exactly the same plain design as the slave beds in the villa at Civita Giuliana. Scrunched up at the head was a piece of material that probably served as a pillow. Beside it was a wooden chest, divided into two compartments. During the eruption it was emptied save for a clay lamp, a plate and a piece of fabric (clothing, perhaps?); the lid was off, leaning against one of the walls. Beside the door was what we named the 'kitchenette': a roof tile on the floor with traces of fire. Here the inhabitants could warm themselves up a bit with the coals from the kitchen fire; maybe there was some spiced wine in one of the little clay jugs that stood on the floor in front of it.

At the rear of the house we excavated a room that perhaps belonged to the same complex, although for the time being this remains speculation. The furnishing is slightly more luxurious here because this is probably in the more prestigious part of the house, where the owners lived. All the same, it's likewise 'small and cramped'. The room, 12 square metres in size, was lit merely by a tiny window above the door. The walls are decorated with simple patterns and the floor is again tamped earth mixed with marl. Two beds and a small cupboard took up more than half the room; we were able to take plaster casts of these too. The items of furniture are significantly more expensive than those in the other room. Wooden panels on the walls protected against the humidity and cold of the masonry; next to one of the beds the panel was decorated with filigree ivory carvings.

The floor had sunk in the middle of the room. To stop the bed from wobbling someone had put a piece of wood under the bedposts; this has also been preserved as a plaster cast.

We must imagine that hundreds of rooms were similarly crammed. The same is true of the workshops and shops that opened onto the streets of Pompeii. You can often see a stone threshold, while sometimes in the plasterwork the course of the wooden staircase that led off from this is visible. Holes for beams are evidence of mezzanine levels, sometimes barely taller than a bunk bed, where people slept or stored their tools and supplies. One such shop, 10 square metres in size, can be found on Via di Nola, to the left beside the entrance to one of Pompeii's largest residences, the House of the Centenary. Holes for beams in the wall show that there was another floor above with a small window looking onto a side street. And yet another. It has been suggested that it was home to a craftsman and his family. Whether this was the case is anyone's guess, but the expansion of a workshop into a sort of residential tower where a maximum number of people and goods could be housed on a footprint of 10 square metres speaks volumes.

The way in which these shops were shut up at night is insightful too. Almost all workshops open up wide, like a garage. The threshold almost always has a narrow track set into the stone into which boards could be placed vertically. On one side the track widens to become a doorstep with a hinge.

What this means can be seen in the Via dell'Abbondanza, where a plaster cast was made of one such 'garage door' as an impression in the ash layer. A night door was inserted in the vertical boards, allowing the inhabitants to go in and out without having to open the entire door. This is very similar to the old palazzi of Naples that have been converted into apartment blocks, university buildings or offices. The huge double doors have a much smaller one inserted into one side; you have to duck when you go through them.

Talking of Naples, with its distinctive *bassi* the city comes surprisingly close to ancient Pompeii. *Basso* means 'deep, low', and the *bassi* are one- or two-room flats with low ceilings on the ground floors of the palazzi of the nobility and clergy. They were rented, predominantly to their own clientele, in a very similar way to how we must imagine the shops of Pompeii were, which were also mostly part of larger house complexes.

Light and air come only through the door and a small window that is set right beside the door. Many of the *bassi* are still inhabited today. The cramped nature of the space inside, which is often kitchen, living room and bedroom in one, forces people onto the street, which becomes part of the living area. Clothes horses, armchairs, tables, boxes extend along the street; especially in summer, life is lived mainly outside.

It must have been like this in Pompeii too, as the *bassi* there were not complete apartments in the modern sense. In the majority of cases they didn't have kitchens, lavatories or bathrooms.

A CITY ON THE VERGE OF CATASTROPHE

What did the people who lived there eat? We must bear in mind that the lower and middle classes usually didn't cook; they ate bread and that was it. There might be an onion too, olives, perhaps a hunk of cheese, salted fish, nuts and figs, but these were already treats. 'Give us this day our daily bread', as it says in the Lord's Prayer, means that most people had to be content with this.

To have a warm meal, people could go to one of the snack bars (thermopolia). So far more than eighty of these have been excavated, most recently in 2020 in the centre of Pompeii. These places served ancient street food – hot soups and stews to take away. Usually there was nowhere to eat on site and, when there was, space was very limited. Either you took your dish home or ate it in the street.

And how did those without a bathroom at home, which only the richest could afford, wash themselves? Water from one of the public fountains could be used for a cursory wash. A warm bath could be had in public baths, of which there were several in Pompeii: the Stabian baths and the Forum baths, as well as the smaller, apparently privately run Sarno baths and the suburban baths at Porta Marina, where the paintings of couples having sex has led to speculation that a brothel operated on the upper floor. The largest baths complex in Pompeii was never finished. In the city centre an entire block of houses was pulled down to build new baths along the lines of those in fashion in the capital, where the emperor was building baths adorned with marble panelling and statues. But the eruption of Vesuvius intervened; the Central baths have been preserved for modern archaeology as a building site.

Anyone who's visited a hammam, a 'Turkish bath', will understand a Roman baths complex without the need for any further explanation. The principle is the same, and not without reason, for the hammam comes directly from the Roman bath via bathing culture in the Eastern Roman Empire.

The sequence goes from cold to warm. After the changing room, where you leave your clothes (preferably watched over by a slave or a friend, because there was a lot of stealing), comes a room with a cold pool, the *frigidarium*. Then comes a room with lukewarm water (*tepidarium*), followed by a pool that is very hot (*caldarium*). The water in this room could get up to 40 degrees Celsius.

The segregation of the sexes was guaranteed, theoretically at least, by separate wings for men and women. Where it wasn't possible to separate the space, the sexes took it in turns to use the baths.

Fresh water came from the aqueduct. The baths were heated by a large wood-burning stove that was outside of the bathing rooms. From there the warm air circulated via double floors, and often in vertical tubes in the masonry too or in double walls.

The bathing culture of the Romans is frequently described as a luxury and a particular cultural achievement. And it's true, of course, that the baths weren't strictly necessary for survival. Yet the idea of the baths as places of luxury and pleasure falls short. The inhabitants of Pompeii were as unlikely to think of the baths as a luxury as the people in a city like Tabriz in Iran or Quetta in Pakistan, where the ancient culture of the hammam lasted almost unchanged until the 1960s.

In the Islamic world this is connected to the prescribed religious ablutions. But religious considerations aside, just imagine a city like Pompeii, packed with people, some of them living in the most crowded conditions, without general access to personal hygiene. Here we must consider the winter months too. For some reason we tend to imagine antiquity as an eternal summer, inhabited by lightly dressed people in short tunics. The cinema is probably to blame for this: in most sword-and-sandal films the sun is always shining. But in Pompeii it got cold in winter and there was snow on Vesuvius. Even in the large houses with atriums, the damp weather and long rainy days were hard to bear, so what must it have been like in the dark shops with their damp walls and tamped earth floors, on streets that turned into torrents when it rained (Pompeii didn't have an extensive sewer system; this function was performed by the streets)? For many the baths were the only possibility of occasionally warming their frozen bones. And if that didn't work, the only thing left was spiced wine, *mulsum* in Latin. 'When I've downed a cup of *mulsum*,' one of the guests at Trimalchio's banquet says in *The Satyricon*, 'the cold can go to hell!'[44]

And if you needed to go yourself? Larger houses had latrines, usually beside or even in the kitchen. This seems odd to us today. But we must remember that only slaves worked in the kitchens of the rich and no consideration was taken of their sense of smell. The usual solution was the chamber pot, whose contents were often just thrown into the street or onto the nearest dung pile.

The fact that Pompeii had a much larger population than previously assumed, as can be concluded from the inscription discovered in 2017, has consequences not only for life in the houses and streets of the city. We also have to rethink our model of Pompeii as an economic area.

Greeks and Romans always thought of the state, its administration and economy as a city state, as a population centre with an agricultural territory attached. Fundamentally this didn't change when a small, originally insignificant city – Rome – grew into a huge empire. The Roman Empire was conceived as a network of city states with local administration. The institutions of the city of Rome – Senate, consuls, army etc. – had in essence remained the same as those that had existed before Rome rose to become the metropolis of the Mediterranean. Only now it had a sort of oversight of countless other municipalities. The imperial office didn't have any institutional grounding originally either. To begin with, the emperor was simply a politician like any other, except that he unified a particularly large number of offices and titles in his person.

The framework of all economic and political theory was and remained the city state, *polis* in Greek (from where our word 'politics' comes), *civitas* in Latin (which lives on in 'civil', 'civilisation' etc.). Autarky, meaning independence, was already the ideal for the Greeks. In antiquity it was assumed that there could be no political independence without economic independence, a doctrine that is seen as obsolete by those flying the flags of liberalisation and globalisation, even though the topic – in the West's relationship to China, for instance – is ever present. But ideals and reality diverged even in antiquity. The

A CITY ON THE VERGE OF CATASTROPHE

Roman Empire accelerated this process and Pompeii is an outstanding example of it.

The area surrounding Pompeii that could be used for agricultural purposes comprised almost 130 square kilometres. Admittedly this is an estimated figure too, because we don't know the exact boundary lines with the neighbouring territories. But even if the area had been a little larger, it still might not have been sufficient to feed 45,000 people. Although Campania was and is one of the most fertile regions in the Mediterranean, to fill that many bellies more farmland would have been needed.

But that's not all. In the years leading up to the eruption, a substantial proportion of agricultural land, probably more than half, wasn't used to nourish the population at all. Instead of cereals and olive oil, wine was produced for export. Wine amphorae from Pompeii have been found from the south of France to the eastern coast of Spain and from Sardinia to North Africa. They have also been detected in Ephesus, in present-day Turkey. The Vettii, whom we met in the first chapter as nouveau-riche house owners, owed their prosperity to dealing in wine, like many other Pompeians from higher society.[45]

In Oplontis, a small harbour in the area surrounding Pompeii, a distribution centre was excavated that is striking by the standards of antiquity. Known by the rather confusing name 'Villa B', it had more than seventy rooms on two floors and was right on the coast. From here wine from Pompeii was shipped all around the Mediterranean, evidence for which are the sherds of more than 1,300 amphorae that have been found in the region. In the courtyard of the complex, not far from several hundred upturned amphorae, waiting to be reused, was a small oven in which pine resin was melted. This was used to make airtight seals for the amphorae prior to shipping.

Another, not insignificant part of the territory was occupied by luxury villas whose owners came from the highest circles of Roman society. Cicero had a villa in Pompeii, as did the family of Agrippa, the general, friend and son-in-law of Emperor Augustus. Emperor Nero's second wife, Poppaea Sabina, owned a huge private villa not far from the harbour of Oplontis, known as 'Villa A', only part of which has been excavated. This type of land use also reduced the total agricultural land that could have provided food for the local population.

Pompeii thus relied heavily on imports, of basic foodstuffs too. The city couldn't have survived otherwise. Economically the system appears to have worked. The city exported wine and other goods to import cereals that it couldn't cultivate in the necessary volumes. An early example of an interconnected economy that wasn't so dissimilar to our globalised goods cycle, at least at first glance. But a closer look reveals that, beneath the surface of what seems to be a modern, interconnected economy, large swathes of the population lived at a level of poverty and underdevelopment that is hard for us to imagine today. In the mountainous inland regions, but also in the suburbs and the countryside of flourishing centres like Pompeii, time seemed to stand still. The benefits of 'progress' never really reached the groups living in these areas. One of the reasons why this was never properly redressed in antiquity was slavery, which was structurally connected to war and permanent expansion, for only in this way could large numbers of new slaves be added to the system. As long as it continued, the slave trade allowed the

A CITY ON THE VERGE OF CATASTROPHE

elites to increase production without investing in innovation and social development. This is probably why the ancient Romans failed to create an economy that's comparable to a modern one (in the sense of an autonomous social sphere of activity and theoretical field).[46] And presumably that's also why the end of Roman expansion in the second century CE (a century later) led to an economic decline that in the long term spelled the collapse of the ancient world.

Notwithstanding this later development, in the first century CE, when Rome's economy was still flourishing, Pompeii grew too – demographically, economically and in terms of its urban development. What was already the reality in Rome, the ancient megacity, repeated itself here on a small scale. Rome was dependent on grain imports from North Africa to feed its population.

When at some point in Pompeii's history, probably in the first half of the first century CE, the number of people living here overtook the number of those who could live off the produce from the surrounding area, possibly nobody noticed at first. It was only when imbalances emerged in the complicated Mediterranean network that this early form of globalisation showed its dark side.

Supply shortages, severe weather, drought and social unrest in remote regions of the empire could lead to price fluctuations that threw Pompeii's system off balance. This happened at least once during the lifetime of the aforementioned Gnaeus Alleius Nigidius Maius, whose grave inscription has allowed us to estimate the population of Pompeii. Among the good deeds of the dead man is his mitigation of a grain shortage that lasted four years and which hit hardest those at the bottom of society. Alleius Nigidius Maius bought grain at the price of five denarii a bushel, then sold it on to the people at three victoriati (corresponding to about 1.5 denarii). He also had bread distributed to the people *per amicos suos* ('by his friends'), meaning the network of clients, ex-slaves and friends who gathered in the atrium every morning.

It seems extraordinary that in one of the most fertile regions of the Mediterranean a four-year food shortage could occur in peacetime, which could only be counteracted by a 'grain discount' financed by a local politician. On the other hand, maybe it's not so astonishing, considering how the war in Ukraine, for example, is threatening the grain supply of even those countries that traditionally produced a surplus. In spring 2022 the German Institute for International and Security Affairs suggested that as a consequence of the war the grain shortage would have a particularly drastic effect on North Africa, i.e. on one of 'Rome's granaries' that once upon a time helped supply large parts of the empire.

CHAPTER FOUR
WHAT COUNTS IN THE END

Maria Rispoli says that after the day which could have been her last she rearranged her priorities. At the time she was nineteen and had grown up in Castellammare di Stabia, surrounded by Roman villas and the everyday hardship of life in a small town to the south of Naples, in the stranglehold of the Camorra, omertà and criminality. One day she found herself in the thick of it, purely by chance: a hostage in a bank robbery, a pistol to her head for eighteen minutes. Then everything happened very quickly. The person holding her hostage was shot dead and another person in the group opened fire on her. She stood there, rooted to the spot, until another hostage, a young man, grabbed her by the arm and pulled her to the floor. Thirty bullets flew past her, some whistling through her hair. Her life flashed before her. This is it, she thought. But she survived, unscathed. She tied the knot young and gave birth to a daughter while she was still studying archaeology. These days Maria works at the Archaeological Park in Pompeii. 'It's always been my dream,' she says, 'to bring about change through our work in this region.'

I think she's the right person for the project I consider to be the most important of my first year in Pompeii, but which barely anyone seems keen on to begin with. Theatre involving young people from the region at the World Heritage Site of Pompeii? What's the point, what's it got to do with archaeology and heritage conservation? Nobody says this in so many words, but the looks at our team meetings are telling, more so than the guarded silence.

Later, after the premiere of the sold-out production in the ancient theatre of Pompeii in May 2022, Maria tells me she understood the point of it from the very beginning. But she wondered why I was doing it. Why was I interested in their problems, in the young people from the periphery of Naples, given that I had a very different background?

My thoughts return to my first days as the director of Pompeii at the start of April 2021. Italy is in pandemic lockdown and the park is closed to the public. The announcement of my appointment is a month and a half old. Six weeks of sustained bombardment and no end in sight. On the day of the official announcement by the Minister of Culture, two members of the academic advisory board resign in protest at my nomination. Too young, too inexperienced. One hundred and forty professors and former curators sign a petition against my appointment. I've never read the list of the signees but have found out a few of the names through friends. Some I knew personally, in certain cases for a long time. Anonymous letters arrive at the office in Paestum, accusing me or colleagues of being corrupt, incompetent and criminal, copied to the office of public prosecution, the police and the local press.

WHAT COUNTS IN THE END

A small group of frustrated pensioners and professors home in on a project that prior to my departure for Pompeii I undertook in Velia, an old Greek colonial city that has been part of the Paestum archaeological park since 2020. In antiquity it was known for its salubrious climate. The city's ancient theatre (beautifully positioned among old olive trees with a view of the sea) had been restored in 2000, gaps in the ancient rows of seats filled in with lime mortar. When in 2020 as director of Paestum I also assumed responsibility for Velia we made the theatre one of our priorities. For there were cracks everywhere in the mortar, in which vegetation was taking hold, endangering the stability of the original sandstone seats. What's more, although the theatre was restored twenty years earlier, it wasn't accessible to the public. Throughout my time in heritage conservation I've repeatedly been amazed by cases like this, which are not that rare. A monument is restored then closed to the public.

In Velia they were so wedded to this approach that the sides of the seating, more than 3 metres high, weren't secured by railings. Which meant that visitors, particularly those with small children, couldn't be left near the ruins of the theatre because of the danger of a fatal fall.

The upshot of this was that the theatre could no longer fulfil its original purpose as a performance venue. The brilliant acoustics of the construction remained hidden to the public too. When we went to Velia with our children for the first time we sat (although it was still prohibited at the time) on the steps and marvelled at this wonder of ancient architecture. Anyone who stands in the centre of the orchestra, the round area that serves as a stage at the bottom of the semi-circular seating, can be heard clearly all the way to the back rows, even if they whisper.

Apart from an overhaul of the restoration work from 2000, our project thus included the installation of railings so that every visitor to Velia, young or old, could enjoy this experience.

Even today I still don't really understand why this project became the bone of contention. It was probably a combination of events. A – not especially flattering – photograph of the building site during lockdown, with boards lying around, was leaked to the press. The retired architect who'd restored the theatre in 2000 posted comments on Instagram in which he criticised our decisions without knowing the project in detail. Eventually a member of the Italian Senate jumped on the bandwagon, and thus the theatre at Velia became the subject of debate in the Italian parliament, although to me it seemed like it was just an excuse for the senator to launch a tirade against the Minister of Culture.

It was pure mudslinging, probably a tried-and-tested formula, but it astonished me all the same. Someone levels an accusation, any old thing, even if it's pure invention. Some local paper prints it, which gives the story a sense of reality; it's in the paper after all. If I don't comment, that must mean it's true. If I do answer, it shows I'm taking it seriously. And so there must be something to it.

The senator, for example, began her tirade in parliament with the insinuation that the restoration of the theatre at Velia (which cost approximately €130,000) had been undertaken without the approval of the relevant antiquities department and had been entrusted to a firm that lacked the necessary expertise, bypassing the normal tender procedure. None of this was true. But once put out there, such accusations circulated and it took months until all the analyses, reviews and investigations that got under way were complete. With the result that . . . none of it was true. Every aspect of the project was vetted, the state authority came on several occasions to carry out site inspections and a surveyor was even called to measure the theatre again single-handedly. If you add up what all that must have cost, it would have probably been enough to restore the theatre again.

It felt like the aim was to make me look incompetent and criminal, i.e. someone who under no circumstances ought to be entrusted with Pompeii. And even though I was certain we'd done everything correctly in Velia, it was a hard time nonetheless. Because you never know how something like that will turn out, and depending on how it goes you can be so badly discredited that you eventually see yourself as a burden – for the ministry and the park. And if the shit really hits the fan, it doesn't much help if later it turns out to have been nothing. By that time you've already gone or been given the boot.

The shit didn't hit the fan. But it wasn't easy. Pompeii required all my energy and at the same time I had to grapple with the accusations over Velia. I noticed my head wasn't always in the right place, and nor was I there for my wife and children, who were seven and twelve at the time. I needed a strategy.

To begin with I decided to stop reading the press review from the ministry that arrives every morning by email. This spared me updates on the petition against my appointment and comments about the theatre at Velia from people who had never been interested in it in the past, but now suddenly behaved as if they were concerned experts. I asked a friend, a journalist by trade, to look through them for me and only let me know if there was something really important I ought to respond to.

I made a lot of telephone calls to friends.

I walked every mountain path around the village.

I listened to a lot of music: Vladimir Horowitz, Oscar Peterson, Keith Jarrett and Ai Kuwabara, a Japanese pianist. There is a live recording of her in a trio playing a piece entitled 'Somehow It's Been a Rough Day', and that's how most days felt to me, but the nine minutes of music somehow gave everything a structure. Raw but not hopeless. I played some piano every evening too, usually jazz standards or Schumann's 'Scenes from Childhood', up and down the keys. Suddenly these thirteen pieces, including 'Dreaming', no longer reminded me of the geraniums on my godmother's balcony, as they once had, but felt ingeniously childlike, redemptive and expressing warmth.

Irina, Viktor's wife, died. The two of them have ten children, the youngest of whom was three months old at the time. All of a sudden the theatre at Velia and the press review were unimportant.

I got a copy of the New Testament, in Greek, to have something else to read beside restoration plans and files. I found the following verse fitting as a dictum for this time: 'Take therefore no thought for the morrow: for the morrow shall take thought for the things of itself. Sufficient unto the day is the evil thereof' (Matthew 6:34). Live and work as if every day is your whole life; who knows what tomorrow will bring.

WHAT COUNTS IN THE END

And so: What is useful for Pompeii, what can I initiate today that will flourish tomorrow too, irrespective of what happens to me?

A few priorities that set the course to follow.

Use modern technology to get a better understanding in real time of what's happening on the site. Then, on the basis of this, define processes that make it possible to react quickly and flexibly to the observed changes. Drone flights over the whole area every month, as well as after extreme weather events, which are disastrous for the ancient walls but are becoming more frequent as a result of climate change. Currently we are working on using artificial intelligence to evaluate the images. Where is something happening, where should we intervene, before damage occurs to the monuments?

Open the archive using digital platforms. Present the park as a research centre, allow people to share in the complexity of archaeological and restoration work. Hold an open day for people to visit sites of restoration and excavation.

Transform the green areas, gardens and olive groves of the ancient city, which swallow millions every year in maintenance costs, into something of value for the public and the park. We began with the ancient vineyard, where wine is being produced again, and 150 sheep that have been mowing the grass for free in the unexcavated part of Pompeii.

But something was missing. In the years of the Great Pompeii Project it's undeniable that Pompeii became a beacon in a positive sense. Today we're trying to translate this success into a sustainable model so that in the future there will no longer be a need for EU special funds and large-scale projects to 'save' Pompeii.

Paradoxically, however, Pompeii's success also threw into sharp relief the isolation of places in the surrounding area. The brighter the beacon of Pompeii shone, the more apparent it was that the ancient city was a small island in a sea of suburbs and industrial sites, many of them deserted. The only things that seemed to be growing here were youth unemployment and crime rates.

'Pompeii's lovely, it's just a shame about its surroundings . . .' is a phrase I hear often. Politicians are hoping that the archaeological park, by means of a 'strategic plan for the environs of the UNESCO World Heritage Sites of Pompeii, Herculaneum and Oplontis', will help bring about change. But how will this work in practice? Many people who live in the surrounding area see Pompeii as an alien entity that has little or nothing to do with their reality apart from the opportunity to earn some money working in the souvenir shop, as a car park attendant or cleaner in one of the few hotels (many tourists spend the night in Naples and only come for a day trip). Quite a lot of them have never visited ancient Pompeii even though in some cases they only live a few hundred metres from the park. Others last came here on a school trip decades ago.

The 'strategic plan' included a few sentences – less than half a page – on a workshop to introduce young people to the value of preserving sites of historical interest. But before bombarding young people with facts and values, I thought, it was first necessary to create an emotional connection to Pompeii. Something to give them the feeling that they're also part of Pompeii, that the ancient city belongs to them too.

In other disciplines such as ethnology they talk of the 'ethical turn'. I think that all of us working in museums need something like this, including a site like Pompeii, a place of European roots. Put very briefly, the 'ethical turn' can be formulated thus: museums are not simply places where people make connections between objects via wall texts and apps, but spaces where objects create connections between people. Pompeii as a place of encounters between people, some long vanished, others full of life – that's it.

Maybe the theatre at Velia was the driving force behind the idea or, having been so exasperated by the whole affair, my determination to get something positive out of it too. After all, the most beautiful marsh marigolds can grow on sludge. At any rate, one day on my way back home from work it occurred to me that theatre was the solution.

Ancient Pompeii had two theatres. The smaller one, also called the Odeon, was roofed, whereas in the larger one people sat in the open air. As protection against the summer sun, sails could be attached to long poles. The large theatre goes back to the second century BCE, which means it was already about 200 years old at the time of the eruption of Vesuvius. In the time of Emperor Augustus (ruled from 31 BCE to 14 CE) it was completely refurbished, as an inscription recalls. The refurbishment was financed by two members of the Holconii family which – how could it be any other way – also had a hand in the lucrative wine business.

The theatre is one of the first buildings to have been excavated at Pompeii. Large sections of it were uncovered as far back as 1765. It had room for up to 2,000 spectators. Since the 1980s it has been used once again as a performance venue for classical and contemporary theatre. But Frank Sinatra and Nina Simone appeared here too. In 2022 we played host to Patti Smith.

The idea was that young people from the area around modern Pompeii would perform in the same time-honoured theatre. And that the usual middle-class audience from Naples and Salerno would be joined by these young people's family and friends.

Performing drama means being fully involved. There is no other way. Everyone is dependent on everyone else; this isn't learning for school but for life, even if it's parents and siblings in the audience, as I remember from my schooldays.

In the Italian school system there's little space for this, sadly. The curriculum is strongly geared towards content, which not infrequently ends in learning facts, dates and terms by rote. Creativity and active participation are less called for. There are exceptions, of course, but most of these depend on the initiative of individual teachers.

The project took place nonetheless, but it wouldn't have been possible without the efforts of two people. One was Luisa Franzese, the head of the senior school authority for the region of Campania, whom I knew from my time in Paestum. She made it possible for the schools to participate in the first place, despite all manner of bureaucratic hurdles. We began with two schools: a *liceo* (a more academic school) in Pompeii and an *istituto professionale* (a vocational school) in Torre del Greco, situated on the coast between Naples and Pompeii. In this way we intended to bring together young people who otherwise had nothing to do with each other.

The other person was Antonio De Rosa, a Neapolitan who ended up in Ravenna in northern Italy, where he works as the director of the Ravenna Festival. One of our problems was that, as archaeologists, we had no idea how to produce a play, let alone how to work with young people as actors.

I knew Antonio because we'd organised a concert together with the Ravenna Festival in Paestum, in the shadow of the monumental Temple of Neptune. Riccardo Muti conducted the Cherubini Orchestra. I made friends with Antonio, Riccardo and his wife Cristina Mazzavillani, and decided to ask for help with the theatre project in Pompeii. For this wasn't going to be the usual school drama, but 'proper' theatre under the leadership of professional artists.

And so my first work trip as director of Pompeii took me to Ravenna. Many eyebrows were raised in the ministry in Rome. Weren't there more important things to do in Pompeii? When I told the head of our finance department how much money we needed to budget for the project he had difficulty stifling his horror. We were rebuffed by the sponsors we approached; they preferred to give money for exhibitions and restoration projects.

One afternoon in April 2021 we sat in Antonio's office in Ravenna, working through various ideas. Classical theatre? Musical theatre? Dance? How far would a template have to be adapted to achieve something worthy of performance with the youngsters within an academic year?

Antonio and his team made me aware of all the difficulties associated with such an undertaking. At the end of the meeting, which I found pretty discouraging, they suggested I contact Marco Martinelli, who worked at the Ravenna theatre and who in 2006 had undertaken a project with young people from so-called problem areas in Naples. Marco said he had about half an hour spare the following morning.

And so it began. As assistant directors Marco got two of the young people who'd been part of his project in Naples and subsequently become actors: Valeria Pollice and Gianni Vastarella. Masks and costumes: Roberta Mattera. Lighting: Vincent Longuemare. Music: Ambrogio Sparagna. The play was Aristophanes's comedy *The Birds*. Together with the actors, seventy in total, Marco worked on an adaptation of the material, all about Athens in the fifth century BCE, stricken by plague, war, mismanagement and corruption. But it also became about Pompeii, Scafati, Torre del Greco and Torre Annunziata, and what it's like for a young person to live there in a time of pandemic, the Camorra and economic emigration.

Marco did fantastic work. He gave everybody the feeling that they were being taken seriously. Anybody doubting this can see the documentary film that Marcello Adamo made about it. He followed the youngsters from day one, interviewing some of them at regular intervals.

At the beginning of the theatre project, many of the students said that there was no way they'd be coming back. But most did return. None had ever heard of Aristophanes. And no one had visited Pompeii of their own accord. Quite a number of the participants, who were between fourteen and seventeen years old, were already working because their families could barely support them or not at all. Some had to take time off to attend rehearsals. One boy who was seventeen was about to become a father. Others had to be persuaded not to turn up stoned to rehearsals.

I'm still in contact with many of them today. Some come to exhibitions and tours through the excavations, and a few haven't missed any of the performances that the Naples theatre organises in summer in Pompeii. The teachers say their pupils have changed. A few who were struggling academically didn't have to repeat their school year after all. A girl who was too shy even to utter her name at first took a speaking part. The father-to-be was invited to a casting by a professional theatre shortly before he went to Germany for a few months to earn money in the kitchen of an Italian restaurant in Eisenach.

The premiere was on 27 May 2022. Many of the young people were in tears – beforehand because they were scared by the packed auditorium, and afterwards because now it was all over. There were tears in my eyes too, the whole evening, but nobody noticed because I was sitting in the front row. Although I'd sometimes been there during rehearsals, what I saw was simply staggering. The acting was so good that I didn't recognise many of the youngsters on stage. Teenage girls and boys had been transformed into actors declaiming their view of Athens/Naples. The theatre in Pompeii had become their theatre.

The title of the project came from Maria Rispoli: *Sogno di volare*, which pretty much means the 'dream of flying', but also

'I dream of flying'. I didn't think much of it at first, but then again I didn't have a better alternative. In the end I found it very apt. For the press conference we made badges that said *Sogno di volare*. Some staff still go around wearing them now.

Together with Marco we decided to repeat the project in the coming years. We've already found our first sponsor too. So it does work!

Marco couldn't suppress a grin when the first important discovery during my time at Pompeii was made public, in July 2021. Because through it we learned of a man called Marcus who'd organised 'Greek and Latin spectacles' in ancient Pompeii. What a good omen that was for Marco's Aristophanes production.

Marcus Venerius Secundio died at the end of the 60s or beginning of the 70s in the first century CE and was buried in the necropolis outside the Sarno Gate in Pompeii. His grave, which was excavated in 2021 by a team of Spanish archaeologists under the leadership of Llorenç Alapont Martin in conjunction with the archaeological park, is extraordinary in two respects. First on account of the grave inscription, second because of the burial rite.[47]

The inscription, which provides information about his life and the spectacles he sponsored, was emblazoned on a marble plaque in the gable of the small, rectangular funerary precinct, so that it was visible to everybody leaving the city through the Sarno Gate. The lower part of the grave façade was painted with green plants on a blue background; sadly only a few remnants of this have been preserved. But the inscription, carved into the stone, is easily legible:

M(ARCUS) VENERIUS COLONIAE
LIB(ERTUS) SECUNDIO AEDITUUS
VENERIS AUGUSTALIS ET MIN(ISTER)
EORUM, HIC SOLUS LODUS GRAECOS
ET LATINOS QUADRIDUO DEDIT
Marcus Venerius Secundio
freedman of the city, guardian of the Temple
of Venus, Augustalis and adjunct to these.
On his own he put on Greek
and Latin spectacles over four days.

The text may be short but the information we can glean from it is rich. For the first time we have proof of the existence of public slaves, that's to say slaves who were owned by the city of Pompeii. The ancient version of an employee in public service. For Marcus Venerius Secundio is *colonae libertus*, a freed ex-slave of the colony.

Pompeii is described here as *colonia* because after the Social War General Sulla ordered the city to accommodate a colony of Roman veterans. This was 80 BCE. It was only then that Latin became the official language of the city. Prior to that Oscan was spoken, the language of the Italian tribe who'd settled in inland Campania. The settlement of a colony of veterans didn't just mean that the newcomers acquired properties and land, the name of the city was changed too. From now on Pompeii was officially called *Colonia Cornelia Veneria Pompeianorum*, 'Venus colony of the Pompeians'. Venus was Sulla's tutelary deity, which might explain why he integrated her name into that of the city.

Sulla, who'd had hundreds of political opponents murdered and finally had himself appointed dictator, was already a controversial figure in antiquity. Which makes it all the more surprising that the official name he'd given to Pompeii was still in use almost 150 years after his death in 78 BCE.

This is also evident from Marcus's name. Slaves, it must be noted, were regarded as things rather than persons. For this reason they didn't have full names like Roman citizens, which consisted of three parts: *praenomen* (first name), *nomen gentilicium* (family name or, more accurately, clan name) and *cognomen* (literally 'byname', a sort of nickname, although it was often passed down like a family name). If we take Gaius Julius Caesar, Gaius is the first name (if families with lots of children ran out of ideas they simply numbered them: Secundus is the second, Quintus the fifth etc.; the full name of the poet Horace, for example, was Quintus Horatius Flaccus). Julius is the family name of the *gens Iulia*, the Julian clan, which dated back to before the founding of Rome. According to ancient legend, Julus was the son of Aeneas, the Trojan prince and forefather of the Romans. Finally, Caesar is a nickname, which might have something to do with *caedere*, 'to cut out'.

Let's take another example: Marcus Tullius Cicero. Marcus is the first name, Tullius designates his membership of the Tullia family, who came from the small town of Arpinum in southern

WHAT COUNTS IN THE END

Latium, and so couldn't compete with the Julian clan in terms of fame and tradition. 'Cicero' probably comes from *cicer*, which means chickpea. Apparently one of Cicero's ancestors had a chickpea-sized wart on his nose. The classical writer Plutarch tells us that friends tried to persuade Cicero when he was younger to drop the unflattering name, to no avail.[48]

Because the background or family of a slave was irrelevant in antiquity, one name sufficed. Tiro, for example, was the name of a slave who served as Cicero's secretary. This in itself was progress from earlier times when some slaves didn't have names at all. For example, Marcus's slaves were simply called Marcipor, which comes from *Marci puer*, and literally means 'Marcus's boy'.

The slaveowner was, moreover, at complete liberty to change a slave's name at will. This could occur either as a punishment or to express a particular relationship of loyalty.

When a slave was freed it was like a rebirth. The idea behind this was that although slaves had arrived in the world biologically, they did not exist socially. In the eyes of the ancient elites, a slave was essentially nothing more than a 'tool that could speak'. The fact that such a devaluation of human life wasn't just generally accepted but also seen as natural is perhaps the thing we find most disturbing about antiquity. Even an intellectual giant like Aristotle didn't have a problem denigrating slaves as 'inherently' different from freemen.[49] In light of such comments do we have to revise our opinion of the ancient philosopher? Maybe. But we should also ask ourselves which errors of judgement later generations will accuse us of in the future. For example, the contradiction between the declaration of 'universal human rights' by some of the most powerful states in the world and the creation of an economic order that in many cases seems to flout these human rights. In the debate about this we can see how economic structures are repeatedly presented as market driven and virtually without any alternative – in other words 'natural'. How future archaeologists will judge this when they excavate, perhaps, a textile factory in Bangladesh where clothing for the global market is manufactured in inhumane conditions, nobody can now say.

Because the 'tool that could speak' became a new person when they were freed in antiquity, the slave usually took the first name and surname of their former master, as if they were a descendant of the family. The name the slave had been called then became the *cognomen*. Thus when he was freed in 53 BCE Cicero's slave Tiro (around fifty years old) became Marcus Tullius Tiro.

What happened when the city was the slaveowner we can see from our example. Secundio, as he must have been called as a slave, became Marcus Venerius Secundio, to show that he'd been a slave of the *Colonia Veneria*. We don't know why Marcus was chosen as his first name.

The same name crops up in a totally different context in Pompeii: in a receipt for a lease payment received by the banker Lucius Caecilius Iucundus. In 1875, 151 folding wooden tablets were found in his house in Via del Vesuvio, one of the main streets in Pompeii, on which were recorded lease and sales contracts. They were written in wax, although in many cases the stylus carried through to the wood beneath. On tablet 139 a certain M. Venerius Sec. signed as a witness for a transaction.

WHAT COUNTS IN THE END

This must have been between 52 and 62 CE as the tablets date from this time.[50]

Marcus Venerius Secundio's grave inscription expresses pride at the fact that he made something of himself. It goes beyond the usual formula (name, offices, sometimes age reached) but doesn't match the verbosity of Gnaeus Alleius Nigidius Maius's grave inscription that we saw in the previous chapter. Nor does it drift into complexity like an inscription from the necropolis outside the Nocera Gate. That grave, numbered 23OS, is a small shrine that contains statues of the dead whose names are given in an inscription, among them a friend of the family named Faustus. Somebody, maybe the very owner of the tomb, felt the need to add the following text beneath:

> Stay a while, stranger, if it is not too much trouble, and learn what you should avoid: this, as I'd hoped, friend – he accused me, took me to court and a verdict was reached; I thank the gods and my innocence that I was relieved of all trouble. But let not the home gods or gods of the underworld accommodate whomsoever lied about our matter.[51]

Marcus Venerius Secundio restricted himself to a very concise enumeration of what he considered to be the most important achievements of his life. First a string of offices, from the most important to the least significant. *Aedituus Veneris* means guardian of the Temple of Venus, the patron goddess of Pompeii, whose name he incorporated into his own when he was set free. *Augustalis* means member of the order of Augustales who were responsible for the cultic veneration of the emperor. This was one of the few offices open to a freedman. Only the sons of freedmen could apply for most political offices and priesthoods as they'd been 'born free' unlike their fathers born into slavery.

But very few freedmen acquired the wealth necessary to join this exclusive club; you had to dig deep into your pockets. Once appointed, which required an appropriate celebration, the role of an Augustale included a financial obligation besides the prestige attached to it.

The ancient word *minister*, on the other hand, has little in common with our 'ministers' as it simply means helper, assistant – in this case for the same Augustales that Venerius Secundio later became a member. The 'ministrant' in the Catholic Church, which derives from the same Latin term, is closer to the ancient meaning. It's probable that Secundio performed this role before being set free, as such auxiliary work was generally left to slaves. All in all, a remarkable career for a man who'd once been the 'property' of the Pompeii city administration.

The Latin word for slave was *servus*, 'servant'. Our term 'to serve' comes from it, as does the Bavarian greeting of 'Servus', which originally meant something like 'your servant'.

In recent times there has been an impassioned discussion among historians over whether the word 'slave' ought to be used to render the Latin *servus*. The debate has its origins in the

WHAT COUNTS IN THE END

US, where descendants of people who were enslaved until the nineteenth century have pointed out that the term 'slave' reduces the very identity of these people to their dehumanisation through the slave trade.

When I suggested the title 'Slaves and Freedmen in Pompeii' for a lecture at the British Museum in London, I was asked whether I wanted to replace 'slaves' with 'enslaved people'. I consciously stuck with 'slave' for the lecture as well as for this book, however. Although I fully understand why the term should be avoided in the case of people whose descendants are still suffering the consequences of slavery and racism, I find it absurd to begin with antiquity, where the slave markets of Rome were also peopled with white people from central and northern Europe. It would be a pure exercise in politically correct terminology benefiting nobody (who knows if their own ancestors were slaves or freedmen in antiquity, or even both?) and contribute nothing to the real issue, which is coming to terms with modern slavery.

The greatest surprise was the last part of the inscription on Marcus Venerius Secundio's grave: 'On his own he put on Greek and Latin spectacles over four days'. This means that he unilaterally covered the costs for the four-day spectacle. But what might we imagine Greek and Latin spectacles to have been? The word can refer to both athletic competitions and acrobatic acts as well as music, dance, mime or theatre performances. But as the inscription describes them as 'Greek and Latin' we must assume that language played a role. So it was probably singing or theatre.

Scholars have assumed that in the era of the old Roman Republic, *Ludi Graeci*, 'Greek plays', originally meant theatrical performances in Latin that handled Greek material. This hypothesis sees 'Latin plays' on the other hand as popular farces in the traditional manner.

But even if this is true (which is not certain), in the first century CE the old difference, assuming it ever existed, no longer made any sense. Greek literature had become such an integral part of Latin that Greek material in the Latin language was no longer regarded as anything special. In this period 'Greek plays' could only mean that they were sung or acted in the Greek language.

It had long been suspected that this sort of thing happened in Pompeii but it was never possible to prove it. In the entire eastern Mediterranean Greek was dominant, the universally acknowledged lingua franca. Roman provincial administrators and envoys obviously had to speak Greek, while Roman decrees and laws were translated into Greek.

People from the Greek-speaking east lived in Pompeii too, and many others learned Greek, especially those from affluent families. As we've seen in the first chapter, the entire culture, including the murals, was more Greek than Roman. It's likely that in such an environment people would have enjoyed watching plays in Greek too. Many years ago, moreover, a small engraved token was found that on one side shows the theatre in Pompeii, while on the other the name of the Greek tragedian Aeschylus is scratched in Greek letters. This looks like a sort of ticket for a Greek play in the original language.[52]

The inscription from the newly discovered grave outside the Sarno Gate now gives us certainty. There were Greek performances not only in Naples, the old Greek city founded in the late sixth century BCE by Greek settlers, but in Pompeii too, which was Etruscan, Oscan and finally Roman, but never Greek. Evidently, however, the people liked the sound of the language of Homer and Euripides.

We must also consider that Marcus Venerius Secundio came from very modest circumstances. As well as showing that he'd become a financial success, culturally too he'd reached the heights of the elites of the Roman Empire who were fluent in Latin and Greek. And he wasn't alone in this, for organising a Greek play only made sense if there was an audience for it. All the same, there will have been some people who had difficulty understanding the dialogue. There was something slightly individual and definitely exclusive about the choice of including Greek performances in the programme. Venerius Secundio was presenting himself as a cultural connoisseur, maybe even a bit of a snob, who grinned over Greek puns that would remain incomprehensible to many of his fellow ex-slaves.

The other peculiarity about Marcus Venerius Secundio's grave is the funeral rite. In antiquity there were essentially two possibilities: cremation or inhumation. In the last century prior to the eruption of Vesuvius, however, inhuming, or burying, bodies hadn't really been an option. With the exception of those of very small children, all of the known graves from the time after the settlement of the Roman colonists in 80 BCE are cremation burials. In the graves, we normally find urns with the ashes of the dead. Pompeii thus follows a rule that is typical for the whole of Italy at the time, from the imperial house to the graves of simple citizens and freedmen.

Marcus Venerius Secundio deviates from this rule. Like others from the same period, his funerary monument takes the form of a small, walled enclosure, a little more than 10 square metres in size, where the urns of the grave owner and other family members were interred in the ground with no paving. A large part of the enclosure of Marcus Venerius Secundio's grave, meanwhile, is taken up by a structure we only find here: a rectangular box with rounded corners jutting up to the rear of the tombstone with its inscription and paintings. The space inside this box is only 2.5 square metres; you can't stand up.

But to find this out we first had to gain access to the sealed burial chamber. The only opening, measuring 61 × 67 centimetres, had been cemented over after the burial ceremony. Two restorers from the park had to carefully remove the ancient plaster and break through the wall before we could get a glimpse of what was inside.

As soon as the tomb was opened speed was of the essence. The hermetic sealing of the space, whose floor was made of stones and mortar, meant that the skeleton, which was nestling along one of the walls, was better preserved than any other salvaged in Pompeii to date. There was still some skin with hair on the skull. Close-cropped grey hair. The age of the dead man was fixed at around sixty, which tallied with the hair colour and the clearly advanced hair loss in the crown area. And the ears were preserved too. For Pompeii such preservation conditions are truly extraordinary.

They were due to the relatively stable temperature and humidity in the hermetically sealed space. Substances might also have been used to embalm the body, which would have helped conserve it. On top of and beneath the skeleton were the remains of a substance that looks like asbestos; as we know, this mineral was used to preserve corpses.

By opening the tomb after almost 2,000 years the climate inside it became unstable at a stroke. The fact the excavation took place in summer, when the temperature and humidity were both particularly high, made things even more complicated. We documented the find as quickly as possible and took the skeleton to an air-conditioned depot in the archaeological park.

We don't yet have the results of all of the scientific analyses of the grave, but it's already clear that here someone chose a funeral rite that was unusual for the time: inhumation (the burial of the intact body) rather than the usual cremation burial.

That same summer another grave was discovered in the enclosure that perfectly fits the usual picture. It's the cremation burial of a woman whose name was marked on a small marble stele on the grave: Novia Amabiles. Perhaps she was the wife of

Marcus Venerius Secundio, although we can't say that with any certainty because there is nothing in the name to suggest so. It's an example, moreover, of the female name form that wasn't in three parts like those of the men. Instead it was composed of the family name (Novia) and the first name (Amabiles, which is another form of Amabilis, literally 'the lovely one').

As unusual as the inhumation might be in Pompeii and beyond, it isn't unique. The most prominent parallel is no less than the Empress Poppaea Sabina, Nero's second wife. We have already met her briefly as the owner of 'Villa A' in Oplontis, not far from Pompeii. She was from the family (*gens*) of the Poppaei, who came from the region of Pompeii and owned property in the city. The House of Menander, one of the most beautiful patrician houses in Pompeii, is attributed to the Poppaea.

Poppaea Sabina died in 65 CE, in the last years of Marcus Venerius Secundio's life, supposedly from the consequences of a kick that Nero is said to have given his pregnant wife during an argument. She must have been in her mid-thirties at the time, although we don't know the exact year of her birth.

But the stories about Nero are another matter. The image we have of him today – mad wannabe artist, fiddling while Rome burned – was drawn by his enemies after his death in 68 CE, and on some points it's demonstrably false. For example, during the

WHAT COUNTS IN THE END

fatal fire in the capital, in which it's been implied he had a hand (supposedly he wanted to make space for his new palace, the Domus Aurea), he probably wasn't in Rome at all. Afterwards he opened his palaces to the many people who were now homeless.

At the beginning of his rule in 54 CE he was extremely popular with the people and the Senate, although his relationship with the latter deteriorated massively over the years, contributing substantially to his downfall. At the same time he became detached from his mother and his mentor Seneca, leaving him increasingly uncontrollable. Poppaea played a role here too. She was actually married to Nero's friend Otho, but Nero, himself married to Octavia, fell desperately in love with her by 58 CE at the latest.

Reasons of state, embodied by his powerful mother Agrippina who'd placed him on the throne, and the philosopher Seneca, demanded that he remain faithful to his wife. For Octavia was a biological daughter of the Emperor Claudius, while Nero – through the marriage of his mother Agrippina to Claudius – was merely his stepson.

The only thing Nero could think of was to get his mother and Seneca out of the way. Agrippina was murdered in 59 CE; Seneca took a step back from public life and Nero forced him to commit suicide in 65 CE. Octavia was also one of Nero's victims when he accused her of adultery, which was probably a complete fabrication, and ordered her execution.

In 62 CE Nero and Poppaea were finally able to get married. That same year Pompeii was hit by an earthquake, which may have been the reason why the imperial couple visited the badly damaged city. An inscription in the kitchen of the House of Julius Polybius, an influential local politician in the last years of Pompeii, is evidence of this visit. Scratched into the plaster, it shows that even years after Nero's violent death and the *damnatio memoriae* decreed by the Senate (the destruction of all official memorial statues and inscriptions for the emperor) he and Poppaea must have remained very popular in Pompeii. In any event it was not deemed necessary to remove the inscription. It runs: 'As offerings Poppaea sent the most holy Venus a beryl, a pearl earring and a giant pearl; when the emperor came to the most holy Venus, where your heavenly feet, Augustus, brought you, there was an immense quantity of gold.' An unparalleled golden oil lamp, which was found in the Venus sanctuary in 1863 and is now housed in the National Archaeological Museum in Naples, probably belongs to the mass of gold with which Nero filled the Temple of Venus.[53]

Various 'fake Neros', who cropped up in the eastern part of the empire years after his death, likewise testified to the lasting popularity of the fiddling emperor. There he was admired as a devotee of all that was Greek, especially literature and music. Not only did Nero bring many Greek artists to Rome, he also sang publicly in Greek himself, including in Naples, to the horror of the senators.

Marcus Venerius Secundio's organisation of 'Greek shows' can also be seen as a response to Nero's public demonstrations of reverence for Greece. Whereas the senators were of the view that Nero's artistry was unbecoming of an emperor, we have to assume that it appealed to the common people. After the old emperor Claudius, who spent his spare time studying the

WHAT COUNTS IN THE END

Etruscan language and history, Nero and Poppaea came across as young pop stars.

We can only speculate as to why Poppaea's body wasn't cremated but embalmed and buried intact in its grave, 'according to the custom of foreign kings', as the historian Tacitus wrote.[54] The rest of the ceremony, including the procession to the grave and the eulogy given by Nero, who pretended to be deeply sad (he wasn't even thirty at the time), seems to have run according to the usual protocol. It's probable, however, that the inhumation had either been Poppaea's express wish or at least an attempt to comply with what the bereaved imagined her wishes to be.

What could have been the background to such a request? As Poppaea also fell victim to the Senate's condemnation and the official histories drew a similarly negative picture of her to that of her husband, it's especially difficult to say anything about her character and opinions.

The 'foreign kings' probably refers to the Macedonian kings and successors of Alexander the Great. The body of Alexander, the world conqueror from Macedonia in the north of today's Greece, who died in 323 BCE, was embalmed in honey and taken to Alexandria in Egypt. Octavian, later Emperor Augustus, is said to have viewed the mortal remains of his great idol in 30 BCE and even laid a golden diadem on the dead man. Apparently he accidentally broke off a piece of the nose of the corpse, which was now almost 300 years old.[55]

In Poppaea's (and Marcus Venerius's) time, inhumation may have been seen as drawing on a typically eastern, Greek–Macedonian practice. At the same time it anticipated a later development. From the second century CE, it appears that inhumation again became the dominant funeral practice in Italy too. In the early fifth century an author such as Macrobius could describe cremation as something known only from old books.[56] This development was boosted by Christianity, even though it began long before the rise of Christianity and thus should originally be seen as an independent process. The problem is that the ancient sources tell us nothing about reasons behind the trend of inhumation.

It seems that in early Christianity the choice of inhumation was connected to the belief in a bodily resurrection of the dead; death was regarded as a type of sleep. Christianity thus placed itself in the Jewish tradition, which rejected cremation. Although there appear to have been exceptions, as there were later in Christianity, many places in the Torah suggest that cremation was seen as a dishonour and damnation, which is why it could also be carried out as a posthumous punishment. Execution could be followed by the cremation of the person executed, for example.

Without going into sophisticated theological discussions that were already being conducted in antiquity, we can state that inhumation was part of a tradition that not only had different rites from ancient Rome, but also implied a different relationship to death. Along with some modern researchers we could speak of a 'more respectful treatment' of the dead. Something was awaiting them; perhaps the actual thing only came after death.

The anticipation of the coming of the Messiah, until when the dead 'sleep in the dust of the earth' before they 'shall awake', occurs in Daniel (12:2) in the Old Testament, to which Jesus often refers. Common to both is an apocalyptic eschatological end of days, connected to the resurrection of the dead and a sort of last judgement passed on everyone, dead or alive.

To guard against any misunderstanding, neither Poppaea Sabina nor Marcus Venerius Secundio were Christians. Marcus Venerius was a guardian of the Temple of Venus, while as empress Poppaea participated in countless ancient Roman rites. But maybe the two of them belonged to that group of people searching for new ideas at a time when the traditional world of gods was increasingly perceived to be an empty shell and a formality.

In Poppaea's case we even have some concrete evidence. This is not so much her fascination for the ancient art of astrology that came from Babylon and which her enemies reproached her for after Nero's death. Hadn't Emperor Claudius, in good Roman tradition, banished all astrologers from Italy in 52 CE? Of more interest to us is another detail from her life history – also because it comes from a reliable source. The Jewish historian Flavius Josephus (note the family name Flavius, which identifies him as an ex-slave of the later Emperor Titus Flavius Vespasianus) had no reason to praise or to malign Poppaea. Josephus, who met Poppaea to plead personally for the release of his imprisoned compatriots (the plea was granted, the petitioner richly rewarded by the empress), called her 'pious'. According to Josephus, she was responsible for Nero's intervention in favour of the Jewish priesthood in a dispute with the Roman client king Herod Agrippa II.[57] Here too we should take care not to think in terms of religious conversion. All the same, it appears that Poppaea harboured a certain interest in the god from the east who was so different from the Roman and Greek gods with their human figures and their all too human strengths and weaknesses.

However this may be, after the fire of Rome, for which many held her husband responsible, it didn't stop Nero from making a scapegoat of a small sect that worshipped a so-called criminal sentenced to an agonising death on the cross: the Christians. Many of them were burned alive; this was the punishment for arson. It was the first official persecution of Christians, although it was limited to the city of Rome.

In the eyes of posterity Nero's persecution of Christians has assumed far greater importance than it probably ever did in the view of most contemporaries. Christians were considered to be oddballs. Radical demands such as 'but whosoever shall smite thee on thy right cheek, turn to him the other also' met in most cases with blank incomprehension (as it would probably do so today, the only difference being that we somehow know the saying). The sexual abstinence preached by Jesus and Paul was likewise alien to the sensuous mentality of antiquity.

WHAT COUNTS IN THE END

Time and again the fantasy of modern writers has been sparked by the possibility that early Christians lived in Pompeii too. What effect must the ubiquitous erotic frescoes and the ruthless nepotism and corruption in political life have had on them? How did they react to the traditional rites in the temples of Venus, Apollo and Isis? Is a graffito from Pompeii, consisting of the words *Sodom(a) Gomora*, to be interpreted as contemporary criticism of the conditions in the Roman city from a connoisseur of the Old Testament, equating the sinful cities of Sodom and Gomorrah by the Dead Sea, which were destroyed by Yahweh, with ancient Pompeii?[58]

Such a fantasy was played out by the English novelist and politician Edward Bulwer-Lytton, born in London in 1803. *The Last Days of Pompeii*, which was published in 1834 and has been filmed seven times, tells the story of two young lovers, Glaucus and Ione: he rich, she from a poor family. The story contains all the ingredients of a true crime novel, from murder, blackmail, poisoning and defamation to the showdown in the amphitheatre at Pompeii, where at the last moment the erupting Vesuvius keeps the hungry lion away from his innocent victim, Glaucus. The beast senses the approaching danger earlier than the humans and withdraws anxiously to his cage.

Interwoven into the tale, parts of which are set in the House of the Tragic Poet that had been excavated a few years before publication, is the conflict between nascent Christianity, to which Glaucus and Ione convert in the end, and the old 'heathenism', epitomised by the Egyptian Isis priest Arbaces, the archvillain of the plot. His religion is presented as pure masquerade, performed using cheap magic tricks, making Christianity shine even more brightly as the religion of the future.

There's no historical foundation for this central motif of the story, because we have no clear proof of Christians in Pompeii. Although we have evidence pointing to the presence of Jews in the city, including the aforementioned graffito and a wall painting depicting the Judgement of Solomon, there are no traces of the then small group that saw Jesus of Nazareth as the Messiah and which was open to non-Jews too, apart from a controversial charcoal inscription that has long vanished and of which only some sketches remain from the years after its discovery in 1862.[59]

This isn't surprising considering that at the time Christianity was nothing like what it became through the institutionalisation of the Church. For example, of the New Testament canon, only the epistles of Paul (those classified as authentic were written between 50 and 60 CE) and the Gospel of St Mark (around 70 CE) existed at the time of the eruption of Vesuvius in 79 CE. Other writings may have been in circulation but have not survived. The (relatively short) Gospel of St Mark, moreover, consists principally of stories about miracle healings and prophecies, which means it's full of material that, in the eyes of Bulwer-Lytton, was more typical of the ancient Egyptian religion he described as being irrational and encouraging belief in miracles.

Despite this, Pompeii is informative for the understanding of early Christianity. The city provides an insight into the living conditions of a society in which the new religion was able to gain a foothold, to become the state religion three centuries

WHAT COUNTS IN THE END

later. We've seen how the microcosm of city and farmland, which had prevailed in earlier centuries, disintegrated and how this was reflected in Pompeii's population structure and economy. The complexity that emerged, which individuals could no longer fully comprehend (they had to suffer hunger while the city was exporting wine), must have played a key role in creating fertile ground for new and unorthodox ideas.

And yet it's always baffling how radically new and unorthodox these ideas were. For this reason I have to say, paradoxically, that the longer I study antiquity and Pompeii, the more astonishing and incomprehensible it seems to me that a 'criminal' sentenced to an agonising death on the cross (crucifixion was usually reserved for slaves and non-citizens) could unleash such a movement, especially with teachings that ran totally counter to common sense in antiquity.

CHAPTER FIVE
LIFE GOES ON

Another reason why the city fired the imagination of posterity was that the early Christians' constant expectation of the end of the world seemed to have become reality in Pompeii. God's judgement seemed to have fallen on a sinful city – or at least that was how pious men of the Church were still interpreting it in the eighteenth century. 'Many people implored the gods,' the 'heathen' Pliny wrote. 'Others thought there were no gods left and a new eternal darkness had descended on the world.'[60]

But wasn't there another way of processing the catastrophe, lending it a higher sense, transcending death and destruction? And isn't all life subject to death, meaning that Pompeii's destruction is merely a drastic example of the *conditio humana* in miniature, the basic condition of human existence?

A few years before the eruption of Vesuvius Paul wrote to the Corinthians, 'I die daily' (1 Corinthians 15:31). Death and the demise of Pompeii as the norm, as an everyday occurrence. Every day could be your last so do not worry about tomorrow; tomorrow will look after itself. At the time such thoughts circulated even outside of radical currents like Christianity. Already by the Late Republic skeletons had become a subject of art. In Pompeii we encounter them in mosaics and on silver cups. They seem to be calling out to life, 'Enjoy your existence while you can!' You could also put it thus: 'Reorder your priorities in life in the awareness of its finitude.'

In *The Satyricon*, the satirical novel from the first century CE that throws such a distinctive light on life in ancient Campania, this is turned into ridicule when at the banquet the nouveau-riche host Trimalchio lets a silver skeleton dance on the table and recites:

> Poor man is nothing in the scheme of things
> And Orcus grips us and to Hades flings
> Our bones! This skeleton before us here
> Is important as we ever were!
> Let's live then while we may and life is dear.[61]

Whether this is really funny or somehow deadly serious remains an open question. Just like whether the lesson from the history of Pompeii is that simple: remembering what we would prefer to put to the back of our minds, the fact that the end can come at any moment. That life is fragile. That it's not worth chucking it away as it can be taken from us at any time.

Between 3 and 6 June 1974, while excavating the House of the Golden Bracelet, archaeologists came across the remains of three people cowering in a tiny cellar space, where they'd fled during the eruption. Plaster casts were made of the three: two adults and a child, about five or six years old. In the throes of death the child was clutching one of the adults. It was a reasonable assumption that the group, which is exhibited in the Antiquarium of Pompeii, was a family. But DNA analyses showed that all three were male and likely not blood relatives. So not a family, but three people who were thrown together by a twist of fate and who died in each other's company.[62]

But there's more to Pompeii than that. The city is also a story of survival and life going on. If the number of people who lived here was actually as high as suggested in Chapter 3, this also relativises the number of victims. To date, around 1,300 victims of the eruption of Vesuvius have been found. The exact number is not known as during the early excavations remains of skeletons were neither carefully documented nor preserved. But even if this number were to double and more people died in flight on the roads out of Pompeii, we would arrive at roughly between 10 and 15 per cent of the 20,000 inhabitants who lived in the city according to recent estimates. Which means that around 90 per cent escaped the catastrophe and their lives continued.

But not in Pompeii. Emperor Titus, who'd come to power a few months before the eruption, tasked two officials with the reconstruction of the city. For this they were authorised to use the assets of those dead people who didn't have any heirs. Once they got there, however, the officials realised that there was no point in rebuilding Pompeii. The city and its fertile surroundings had been transformed into a grey desert; beneath metres of stone and ash the city was only vaguely identifiable.

The plundering of Pompeii then began. Private individuals burrowed around in their houses, or where they suspected them to be, for possessions they'd left behind. The forum was tackled systematically. Almost all the marble cladding and bronze statues were removed in antiquity and the precious material reused. Generations of looting followed, the traces of which we still find today during excavations. Paupers rummaged around in ash and dust for objects of value, and probably stumbled across dead bodies in the process.

The upper floors of the houses were still identifiable. Over the years, however, the vegetation grew back, drawing incredible vigour from the volcanic soil that returned the plain at the bottom of Mount Vesuvius into a Garden of Eden, where there could be three or four harvests on a piece of land each year.

And with this came . . . oblivion. Although the memory of a vanished city lived on in the place name of Civita (from the Latin *civitas*), after the beginning of the excavations in 1748 it took fifteen years before it was understood that this was Pompeii rather than Stabiae, which was also known from ancient inscriptions.

From 1592 to 1605 the Count of Sarno had a 21-kilometre-long canal built for his mills in Torre Annunziata, which runs through the middle of Pompeii. The canal is still mostly intact; as large sections of it are open, in many places it was tapped to water the fields. Entrances to the underground section, which runs beneath Pompeii, can be seen in various places in the excavation area. When it was built the workers knocked through ancient walls and found statues and coins. But the time was not yet ripe for the discovery of Pompeii; the finds during the construction works led to nothing. The forgetting would continue.

The magnitude of a catastrophe can also be measured by how

LIFE GOES ON

quickly or slowly it is forgotten. Seen like this, there is something comforting too in the forgetting that soon descended on the ancient city in the form of rampant vegetation. The wound closed. The events were certainly preserved in memory through writings by historians such as Pliny, albeit far too tersely for our liking. But at the place itself no monument commemorated the victims, no sacred ban befell the site of the disaster. Nor was a new Pompeii built anywhere, even though that would certainly have been an option. Even Carthage, archenemy of Rome, could rise again from the rubble under Caesar after being razed to the ground by the Romans in 146 BCE and its entire population sold into slavery. In 397 CE an important Church council even took place in the city. At this time the remains of Pompeii had long been grazed by sheep among the olive trees and vines.

Seen like this, Pompeii's history is also a eulogy to forgetting. After all, without forgetting there can be no rediscovery, without decay no recovery and preservation. Essentially there can't be any history without forgetting either, because history always means selecting what is told and what is left out, i.e. forgotten. If there were no forgetting, the past wouldn't be the past but always completely with us, present, actual.

I believe this is true of all of us, not just Pompeii. Nobody has a sure grasp of what was and what will be, but the mixture of remembering and forgetting with which we view our history is in our hands.

July 2022: another tour, more expectant faces. This time it's not the chamber of commerce but twenty young people from our theatre project. It was their idea and of course I agreed. The eagerness in their faces isn't because they finally want to know what Pompeii means and why it's important. They already know that. It's the place where 'their' theatre is, a place they associate with emotions, joyful ones as well as a few painful ones. They're expectant because they want to see how the director talks to them about 'their' place, what there is new to say about it. I don't know precisely. We will go to see the restorers at the House of the Vettii. Maybe I'll tell them about Dionysus and Ariadne or the four styles of Pompeian wall paintings. Or the lives of slaves and freedmen, and their graves, like Marcus Venerius Secundio's. Perhaps they want to know something completely different, we'll see. Where one begins isn't that important. What counts in the end is already inside them.

AFTERWORD

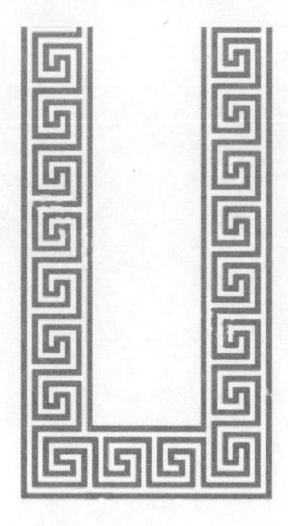

AFTERWORD

A few months after this book was published in its original, German version, Pompeii's largest excavation campaign in a lifetime began. As I am writing this, in and around the ancient city archaeologists are digging through ash layers and pumice stones on roughly 9,000 square metres – a greater area than any that has been excavated in the last sixty years. In Regio IX, a section in the heart of the ancient city, an excavation project aiming at straightening the scarp separating excavated and unexcavated areas in one of the houseblocks, known as insula 10, led to the discovery of stunning new frescoes.

Of course, excavations in Pompeii have been going on for more than two and a half centuries. And besides the examples discussed in this book, such as the Villa of the Mysteries or the House of the Vettii, there are many other houses that have yielded breathtaking artworks. To mention just a few, there is the House of Menander, the House of Loreius Tiburtinus, the House of the Gilded Cupids, the House of the Orchard and the House of Marcus Lucretius Fronto, who may have been a relative of the poet Titus Lucretius Carus, author of a highly philosophical long poem called *On the Nature of Things*.

My colleagues and I sometimes question each other about our 'favourite' houses. It's just a little game we play during a break in our daily routine, and for us it's a bit like being asked as a parent which is your favourite child. However, in such conversations we also remind ourselves of the incredible variety and value of the houses in Pompeii.

Yet, the memory of all these other houses subsides in the magical moment when a new fresco or room comes to light, and we are the first humans to gaze upon it after almost 2,000 years. In such moments, we often catch ourselves thinking: 'this is the most beautiful thing I've ever seen', even though we know that such an impression could not stand up to an objective survey of the thousands of frescoes and rooms discovered in Pompeii.

Among the recent discoveries is a still life on the wall of the hall, or atrium, of a house in Regio IX that almost looks like a pizza as served in modern Naples's pizzerias. Of course, this cannot be: the Romans had neither tomatoes nor mozzarella, essential ingredients for the Neapolitan pizza. Yet, the pitta-like bread with fruits (dates, pomegranates) and spices on it, next to a silver cup filled with wine, is part of the same Mediterranean dietary and agricultural tradition that lives on today.

Simple dishes prepared and eaten by the poor often find their way into high cuisine, and eventually even into poetry and wall painting. Just like pizza used to be a poor people's dish, while today it is on the menu of some of the most expensive restaurants in London or Manhattan, the Pompeian painting plays on the contrast between humble content and costly container (the

AFTERWORD

silver plate on which the pitta lies, but also the very wall decoration that contains the image). In this, the image from the Pompeian wall is comparable to Virgil's Eclogues and to the *Xenia* of Martial, short poems describing this sort of gift given to guests: apparently, the most simple things become the object of highly sophisticated works of art.

In the house next door, which must have been huge and is only partly excavated, we discovered a large dining room. Its walls were painted in black so that the smoke of the oil lamps that were lit after sunset, when guests would gather here for lavish banquets, remained invisible. At the centre of the north and south walls beautiful figures were painted directly on the black ground. On the north side, we see a shepherd, dressed in colourful clothes, typical of Asia Minor (modern Turkey) in the eyes of the ancient Greeks, with a crook and a large dog lying in front of him. He is facing a woman accompanied by a female servant. Between them, an inscription in Greek letters reveals their names: Helen and Alexandros, which is another name for Paris, the Prince of Troy. By escaping to his hometown with Helen, Queen of Sparta in Greece and already married to Menelaus, Alexandros sets off the Trojan War. On the south wall the god Apollo, with laurel crown and lyre, is glancing at a woman sitting on a hemisphere: the omphalos, the centre of the world, which according to the Greeks was located in Apollo's sanctuary in Delphi. At first, we thought she was Pythia, the priestess soothsaying in the god's name. However, given the backdrop of the Trojan War in the other painting, she is more likely to represent Cassandra, a sister of Paris, who refused to have sex with Apollo and was therefore punished by the god: she could foresee the future, but was unable to change it, for nobody believed her. Her sad and meditative expression seems to betray her knowledge that her city will fall, and she, after being raped by the Greek invaders, will be dragged off as a slave to Mycenae where she meets her death. The paintings date to the third style, which means that they were already several decades old when Mount Vesuvius erupted. In several spots, they have been restored and refreshed in antiquity, presumably between the earthquake of 62 CE and the destruction of the city in 79 CE.

Still more frescoes came to light in other excavation sites: in the House of the Painters at Work, the fourth style wall decoration of a tiny cubiculum (bedroom) was preserved right up to the ceiling. The decoration pattern and the artistic quality recall the House of the Vettii. Besides Perseus, Andromeda and Orestes, the mythological scenes on the walls show a small hooded boy with a dog, sitting between huge grapes. In the house next door to the House of Leda, where a new roof is being built to protect the frescoes, right at the edge of the excavation trench a mythological painting showing Phrixus and Helle came to light. We see the siblings escaping from their stepmother, who conspired to kill them, crossing the strait between Europe and Asia riding on the ram with the Golden Fleece. But Helle has slipped down into the sea and is drowning, reaching out vainly with her arm towards her brother, her face already underwater. Henceforth, the strait will be named after her: Hellespont.

However, it is not primarily the paintings that keep coming back to my mind as I recall the months of the 'great dig' of 2023–2024. It's the people. There are those who died during the eruption. Two men were entombed under the collapsing upper

AFTERWORD

floor of a kitchen in the insula of the Chaste Lovers. On the other side of the block, two individuals, maybe a man and a woman, seem to have been desperately seeking refuge in the House of the Painters at Work, but the door was shut and they could not get in. They died in the hot pumice stones, as if they had drowned in them. Their bodies were almost completely submerged in the pumice layer, their positions and gestures indicating that they were struggling to keep afloat. This is a unique situation as far as we know, and will require further analysis. In the house with the 'pizza' fresco, two women and a child in a bakery were buried under debris, their skeletons suffering dozens of fractures. Apart from the work of park anthropologist Valeria Amoretti, who analyses the skeletons to establish sex, age, possible diseases and cause of death, excavating a victim follows the same technical procedures as any other 'finding'. Yet, it's not the same, for in Pompeii we get so close to the stories of the victims, their faces, names, writings, that it's sometimes difficult to bear.

Then, there are those whose traces can still be seen, as if they had just left; who knows whether they made it out? The workmen who left their tools and piles of bricks and tiles in the house with the bakery, where restructuring work was under way. The hollows in the pavement around the mill stones of the bakery where the two women and the child were found; indentations left by the feet of mules and enslaved workers, going round and round the hourglass-shaped mills for hours and days. What was particularly striking was the fact that the only window of this bakery complex that we could document was secured with iron bars, and there was only one door, which opened onto the atrium. Evidently, the enslaved workers who milled the grain and baked the bread were held there in captivity. Every night, the owner would bar the door of the bakery before retiring to his chambers frescoed with Greek myths.

In the insula of the Chaste Lovers, we were stunned to find children's drawings in charcoal on the walls of a courtyard showing gladiators and animal hunts, between amphoras and plant beds for the kitchen garden. One of the little rascals had probably managed to sneak into the amphitheatre to watch the bloody games, and was now eager to illustrate the spectacle to the other kids who were playing in the courtyard. Judging from the drawings, the artist must have been quite young, for the arms and legs come directly out of the heads – a way of representing the human figure that young children still use today. This seems to be confirmed by the outline of a tiny hand on the wall of the same courtyard: one of the children had contoured her or his hand with a piece of charcoal. Judging from the dimensions, they were around seven years old.[63]

What we get to see here is maybe not what we usually expect when thinking about the classical world. 'The Other Pompeii' is the title of an exhibition in the archaeological park on the lives of the poor and enslaved. It opened in December 2023 and features about 200 objects shedding light on the people who spent their lives in the shadow of History with a capital H. Exhibits include the reconstruction of the slave room from Civita Giuliana and iron shackles from the gladiators' quarter. In a way, the exhibition is the second volume to this book.[64] It is also an invitation to continue the discussion. There are many 'other cities' hidden beneath the surface of Pompeii. Currently,

AFTERWORD

we're working on an exhibition focusing on the lives of women and girls from the ancient town and its countryside. Just as we ask different questions from past generations exploring Pompeii and the ancient world, future archaeologists will develop new approaches to map the past. However, they won't do so alone, but as part of the broader development of society. Thus, the 'other Pompeii' emerging from the future is already in the making, and each one of us contributes to it, whether we're aware of it or not. Visiting the site is not only a journey into the past, but also a contribution to the future of memory.

ACKNOWLEDGEMENTS

Narrating the 'other Pompeii' in an exhibition made me fully understand that telling the stories of daily life in the ancient city and its territory (and, to some extent, in today's archaeological site) is always a collective endeavour, starting with co-curator Silvia Bertesago, exhibition designer Vincenzo De Luce and the team who worked intensely for about a year on the project. But books, too, exist not only through and for an audience, but also thanks to countless encounters and conversations the author had, often long before writing a single word. This is especially true in a place like Pompeii, a site of such size and complexity that no single person can ever fully comprehend it.

Some colleagues from Pompeii are named in the book, but I would have needed far more space to explain what each of them does and how much everything we do is teamwork. Besides those named in the text I'd like to thank Ludovica Alesse, Maria Pia Amore, Teresa Argento, Giuseppe Barbella, Maurizio Bartolini, Antonio Benforte, Pina Brancati, Alberto Bruni, Mattia Buondonno, Vincenzo Calvanese, Paola Cataldo, Anna Civale, Domenico Costabile, Mattia De Luca, Mariangela Esposito, Andrea Foti, Arianna Galasso, Stefania Giudice, Elena Gravina, Raffaella Guarino, Aniello Iervolino, Marika Lombardo, Rosanna Mariano, Raffaele Martinelli, Clelia Mazza, Paolo Mighetto, Annapaola Mormone, Olga Nastri, Pietro Oliva, Anna Onesti, Ernesta Rizzo, Tiziana Rocco, Maria Rosa Rosa, Marco Rovito, Alessandro Russo, Antonino Russo, Davide Russo, Paola Sabbatucci, Armando Santamaria, Federica Savarese, Giuseppe Scarpati, Anna Maria Sodo, Arianna Spinosa, Christian Starace, Monica Vassallo, Alessandra Zambrano and Salvatore Zaza.

Many thanks also to Alfio Furnari from the Landwehr & Cie agency and Bettina Eltner from Ullstein Verlag in Berlin, as well as to Kirty Topiwala from Hodder & Stoughton, London, and Karen Levine from The University of Chicago Press. Jamie Bulloch did a wonderful job of translating the text.

My sister Mirjam and my friends Anja and Axel read parts of the manuscript and gave me valuable feedback. Katharina, Carlotta and Gianni were unstinting in their support and most importantly made me understand what counts in the end.

Silvia Vacca, who works in visitor services at the Archaeological Park of Pompeii, took most of the photographs, for which I would also like to express my gratitude.

Thomas Fröhlich checked the manuscript for content; all remaining errors and inaccuracies are my fault.

ACKNOWLEDGEMENTS

Finally, huge thanks to Luisa Cavaliere, Domenico Cavallo and Teresa Giuliani – they know why.

As not all of those listed can read English, here is the international Pompeian version:

HIS OMNIBUS PLURIMAS AGO GRATIS, QUIA
SINE CONSILIO AUXILIOQUE EORUM
NIHIL UTILE ASSECUTUS ESSEM.

NOTES

1 G. Magherini, La sindrome di Stendhal. Il malessere del viaggiatore di fronte alla grandezza dell'arte, 2003.
2 K. N. Cotter, A. Fekete, P. J. Silvia, 'Why Do People Visit Art Museums? Examining Visitor Motivations and Visit Outcomes', Empirical Studies of the Arts 40.2, 2021, pp. 275–95.
3 J. H. Falk, 'Viewing art museum visitors through the lens of identity', Visual Arts Research 34.2, 2008, pp. 25–34.
4 Stendhal, Rome, Naples et Florence, 1826, p. 102.
5 Ibid., p. 101.
6 Pliny the Younger, Letters, Book 6.16.
7 M. Osanna, Pompei: il tempo ritrovato. Le nuove scoperte, 2019, pp. 273-300. On the exact date of the eruption of Mount Vesuvius, which is still a matter of dispute, see P. W. Foss, Pliny and the Eruption of Vesuvius, 2022, pp. 115–148.
8 R. B. Stothers, M. R. Rampino, 'Volcanic Eruptions in the Mediterranean Before A. D. 630 From Written and Archaeological Sources', Journal of Geophysical Research 88, 1983, pp. 6357–71.
9 Pliny the Younger, Letters, Book 6.20.
10 J. W. von Goethe, Italian Journey, entry from 13 March 1787.
11 G. Fiorelli (ed.), Pompeianarum Antiquitatum Historia, Vol. 2, 1862, p. 583.

12 M. Tullius Cicero, Letters to Atticus, Book 1.9.
13 Horace, Epistles, 2, Verse 156–57.
14 One of them may have also been the freedman of the other: cf. B. Severy-Hoven, 'Master Narrative and the Wall Paintings of the House of the Vettii, Pompeii', Gender History Across Epistemologies 24.3, 2012, pp. 540–80.
15 Corpus Inscriptionum Latinarum, Vol. IV, No. 8903.
16 Pliny the Elder, Natural History, Book 7.12.
17 Original translation into German by J. F. Wurm, 1839, S. 2394–97.
18 D. King, The Elgin Marbles: The Story of the Parthenon and Archaeology's Greatest Controversy, 2006.
19 Tre lettere del Signor Marchese Scipione Maffei, 1748, p. 33.
20 Italian Journey, loc. cit.
21 Apuleius, The Golden Ass, Book 11.21. Cf. R. Seaford, 'Mystic Initiation and the Near-Death Experience', in: Psychology and the Classics, 2018, pp. 271–77.
22 Plutarch, Life of Crassus, chapter 33.
23 S. Bertesago, 'Pompei e la Seconda Guerra Mondiale', Pompeii-Commitment – Archaeological Matters. Fabulae 04 (28. 01. 2021), online publication.
24 Pausanias, Description of Greece, Book 8.23.
25 Livy, The History of Rome, Book 39.18.
26 A. Maiuri, La Villa dei Misteri, 1931.
27 Ibid., p. 58.
28 Ibid., pp. 160–69.
29 M. Bieber, 'Der Mysteriensaal der Villa Item', Jahrbuch des Deutschen Archäologischen Instituts 43, 1928, pp. 298–330.
30 M. Recke, '"... besonders schauerlich war die Anwesenheit von Frl. Bieber"'. Die Archäologin Margarete Bieber (1879–1978) – Etablierung einer Frau als Wissenschaftlerin', in: J. E. Fries, U. Rambuscheck, G. Schulte-Dornberg (eds), Science oder Fiction? Geschlechterrollen in archäologischen Lebensbildern, 2007, pp. 209–31.
31 Ibid., pp. 214–15.
32 Ibid., p. 217.
33 Published in German as: P. Veyne, Das Geheimnis der Fresken. Die Mysterienvilla in Pompeji, 2018.
34 Ibid., p. 83.
35 G. Sauron, La grande fresque de la villa des Mystères à Pompéi. Mémoires d'une dévote de Dionysos, 1998.
36 M. Osanna, L. Toniolo, Il mondo nascosto di Pompei. Il carro della sposa, la stanza degli schiavi e le ultime scoperte, 2022, pp. 177–233.

NOTES

37 Strabo, Geography, Book 5.4.8.
38 Il Fatto Quotidiano, 10 November 2021, p. 16.
39 J. Packer, 'Middle and lower class housing in Pompeii and Herculaneum. A preliminary survey', in: B. Andreae, H. Kyrieleis, (eds), Neue Forschungen in Pompeji und den anderen vom Vesuvausbruch 79 n. Chr. verschüttten Städten, 1975, pp. 133–45.
40 M. Osanna, 'Games, banquets, handouts, and the population of Pompeii as deduced from a new tomb inscription', Journal of Roman Archaeology 31, 2018, pp. 311–22.
41 Osanna, Pompei, p. 244.
42 H. Ritchie, V. Samborska, M. Roser, 'Urbanization', ourworldindata.org, September 2018, https://ourworldindata.org/urbanization.
43 G. Zuchtriegel, 'Pompei, una città densamente popolata? Nuove scoperte e analisi GIS', Rivista di Studi Pompeiani 33, 2022, pp. 163–71.
44 Petronius, The Satyricon, 42.2.
45 G. F. De Simone, 'The Agricultural Economy of Pompeii: Surplus and Dependence', in: M. Flohr, A. Wilson (eds), The Economy of Pompeii, 2016, pp. 23–51.
46 Cf. the brilliant analysis by Aldo Schiavone in The End of the Past: Ancient Rome and the Modern West, 2000.
47 L. Alapont Martin, G. Zuchtriegel, 'The newly discovered tomb of Marcus Venerius Secundio at Porta Sarno, Pompeii: Neronian zeitgeist and its local reflection', Journal of Roman Archaeology 35, pp. 1–25.
48 Plutarch, Life of Cicero, 1.2–3.
49 Aristotle, Politics, 1.1254b. On slaves as 'tools that could speak', see Varro, De re rustica, Book 1.17.1.
50 A. Hüttemann, Die pompejanischen Quittungstafeln des Lucius Caecilius Iucundus: Text, Übersetzung, Kommentar, 2017.
51 A. Cooley, M. G. L. Cooley, Pompeii: A Sourcebook, 2004, p. 153.
52 C. Pepe, Scrivere. 'Testi greci a Pompei', in: M. Osanna, C. Rescigno (eds), Pompei e i Greci, exhibition catalogue, Pompeii, 2017, pp. 291–99.
53 T. Opper, Nero: The Man behind the Myth, exhibition catalogue, London, 2021, pp. 188–89.
54 Tacitus, Annals, Book 16.6.
55 Cassius Dio, Roman History, Book 51.16.
56 Macrobius, Saturnalia, Book 7.7.5.
57 Flavius Josephus, Jüdische Altertümer [Jewish Antiquities], Book 20, pp. 189–96.
58 Corpus Inscriptionum Latinarum, Vol. IV, Nr. 4976.
59 E. Tuccinardi, Christian Horrors in Pompeii: A new proposal for the

Christianos graffito. Journal of the Jesus Movement in its Jewish Setting 3, 2016, pp. 61–71.
60 See note 9.
61 Petronius, The Satyricon, 34.10. Translated by W.C. Firebaugh, 1922.
62 E. Pilli et al., 'Analisi antropologico molecolari sui calchi di Pompei', in: M. Osanna, A. Capurso, S. M. Masseroli (eds), I calchi di Pompei da Giuseppe Fiorelli ad oggi, 2021, pp. 235–40.
63 Preliminary reports on these and other excavations are regularly published in the *E-Journal degli Scavi di Pompei*, an online journal set up by the archaeological park of Pompeii in May 2023 with the goal of promptly sharing new data from on-going research on the site: https://pompeiisites.org/e-journal-degli-scavi-di-pompei/
64 S. Bertesago, G. Zuchtriegel (eds), *The Other Pompeii. Ordinary lives in the shadow of Vesuvius*, Catalogue of the exhibition, 2024.

INDEX

Adamo, Marcello 186
Aeschylus 197
Agrippa 170
Agrippina 201
Alexander the Great 203–4
Amoretti, Valeria 225
Amphitheatre viii
Antinous of Bithynia 41
Antiquarium of Pompeii 80, 215
Apollo 34–6, 37, 83, 102
Apollo Belvedere 23–4
Apollo the Citharist 29–30, 34, 36–7, 43, 50, 68, 73–4
Apuleius of Madaura 76
archaeology
  elite lives in 142–3
  media relationships 137–44
  and Pompeii Effect 21
  reasons for studying 10–16
  ritual and religion 90–3, 106
  thefts from sites 126–33

Ariadne 55–6, 59, 79, 80, 101, 102, 118, 125, 126
Aristophanes 186
art
  removal of from Pompeii 71–2
  religious aspects of 68–71, 72–4
  Renaissance understanding of 67–8
  Roman understanding of 67
'Art and Sensuality in the Houses of Pompeii' (exhibition) 45–6, 56
Artemis 34
Athena 70–1, 83
Atticus 32–3
August Boeckh Centre for Antiquity (ABAZ) 48
Augustus, Emperor 170, 183, 203–4

Bacchae, The (Euripides) 77–9, 102

Bacchus *see* Dionysus
baths 165–7
Beloch, Karl 147
Berlin Institute of Classical
 Archaeology 113
Bieber, Margarete 110–13
Birds, The (Aristophanes) 186
British Museum 69–70, 195
Brunetto, Marella 139, 140
Bulwer-Lytton, Edward 207

Caesar, Julius 78
Carmenta 82
Carthage 217
Castellammare di Stabia 129
Catoni, Maria Luisa 45
Central Baths 165
ceremonial carriage discovery
 123–6
Ceres 82, 85, 102, 103
Christianity 75, 76, 102, 115–17,
 204–9
Cicero 31, 32–3, 41, 170
Civita Giuliana 123, 126, 131–6,
 141–2
Clark, Christopher 9
Claudius, Emperor 201
collector syndrome 5–10, 126–7
Crassus, Marcus 78
Croesus 35

Daedalus 54
De Petra, Giulio 97, 101
De Rosa, Antonio 185–6
Delian League 70
Delphi 34, 35, 36
Demeter 76
Dionysus 37, 55–6, 76–80, 101–5,
 110, 114–19, 125, 126
Diophantus 62, 63
Doctor Faustus (Mann) 159

Dörpfeld, Wilhelm 112
Doryphoros of Stabiae 127–9,
 130–1

École Pratique des Hautes Études
 90
economic activity 168–72
Elgin, Lord 69
Elgin Marbles 69–71
eroticism 37–44, 58–9
eruption sequence 25–9
Euripides 77, 102
everyday life 143–4, 160–7, 222–3

Fabricius, Ernst 111
Falacer 82
Fiorelli, Giuseppe 147
flamines 82
Flora 82, 83
Fondo Iozzino 83, 84–5
Forum vii, 30, 83, 165
Foucault, Michel 48–9
Franzese, Luisa 184–5
Frazer, James George 81–2
funeral rites 198–200, 203–6
Furrina 82

Gabii 86, 87–9
Garden of the Fugitives viii, 4–5
gender 44–50
German Archaeological Institute
 86, 111, 112
Giuliani, Luca 15
Goethe, Johann von 29, 72–3, 152,
 161
Golden Ass, The (Apuleius of
 Madaura) 76
Golden Bough, The (Frazer) 81
'great dig' 221–7
Great Pompeii Project 29, 95, 181–2
Greater Mysteries in Eleusis 75–6

INDEX

Greece, classical
   eroticism in 39–41
   idea of 168
   religious aspects of art in 69–71
   in Roman Empire 31–3, 36–7, 195–7
   sexual violence in 56–8

Hadrian, Emperor 37, 41
Hephaestus 82
Hera 91
Heraïs 62–3
Herculaneum 72, 74, 182
hermaphrodism 59–63
Hermaphroditus 44–50, 59–61
historical evolutionism 155–60
History of Sexuality, The (Foucault) 48–9
homoeroticism 40–4, 60–3
Horace 40
House of the Centenary 163
House of the Chaste Lovers 224–6
House of the Citharist viii, 29–30, 36–7
House of the Faun vii, 44, 95, 154
House of the Gilded Cupids 221
House of the Golden Bracelet 214–15
House of the Lararium viii, 161–3
House of Leda vii
House of the Library 95
House of Loreius Tiburtinus 95, 221
House of Marcus Fabius Rufus vii, 43
House of Marcus Lucretius Fronto 221
House of Menander viii, 200, 221
House of the Orchard 221
House of Orpheus 80
House of the Painters at Work 224, 225

House of Romulus and Remus 94
House of Venus in the Shell 95
House of the Vettii vii, 51–4, 56, 59–61, 78, 224
houses *see* residential units
Humboldt University 14–15, 32, 44–5, 48, 113

Icarus 54
Italian Journey (Goethe) 29
Ixion 54

Juno 54
Jupiter 54, 82

Last Days of Pompeii, The (Bulwer-Lytton) 207
Leda 39
Liber 102–3
Libera 103
Livy 103, 104
Lo Cascio, Elio 152
Loeschke, Gerhard 112
Longuemare, Vincent 186
Lucretius Carus, Titus 221–2
Lucretius Fronto, Marcus 221
Lupanar 38
Lydia 35

Maffei, Scipione 72
Magherini, Graziella 3
Maiuri, Amedeo 93–5, 96, 98–100, 106, 107, 108, 109–10, 113
Maius, Gnaeus Alleius Nigidius 151, 171, 172
Mann, Thomas 159
Mars 82
Martinelli, Marco 186, 188
Mattera, Roberta 186
Mau, August 52
Mazzavillani, Cristina 185

Medea (film) 81–2
media relationships 138–42
Mergil, Matthias 46
Minerva 83
Minneapolis Institute of Art 127–9
Minotaur 55
Minos, King 54, 55
Müller, Wolfgang 46
museums/heritage sites
   eroticism in 58–9
   fundraising for 99–100
   and sexual violence as an issue 57–8
Mussolini, Benito 94–5
Muti, Riccardo 185
Myron 37
mystery cults 74–6

Nagel, Natalie 46–7
Naples Chamber of Commerce and Industry (CCI) 5
National Archaeological Museum 38, 202
Natural History (Pliny) 25
Nero, Emperor 200–3, 204–5
Nhat Hanh, Thich 16
Nicoletti, Patrizia 137–8
Niobe 34
Nissen, Heinrich 147
Noack, Ferdinand 112–13
Novia Amabiles 199–200

Octavia, Claudia 201
Odeon 183
Oedipus 35–6, 42
On the Nature of Things (Lucretius Carus) 221–2
'Open Pompeii' website 153
Oplontis 155, 169, 182
Orestes 34
Orodes II, King 78, 79

Orpheus 79–80
Osanna, Massimo 82, 86, 89, 123, 125, 151, 152
'Other Pompeii, The' (exhibition) 226–7
Otho 201
Ovid 31, 50, 61

Packer, James 147
Paestum 14, 99, 133, 137–9, 177, 185
Palatua 82
Pan 59–60
Parthenon Frieze 69–70
Paul, Saint 102, 206, 208, 213
Pausanias 101
Pernice, Erich 112
Persian Empire 35
Pasiphaë, Queen 54
Pentheus, King 77–8
Pironti, Gabriella 90–1, 93
Pliny the Elder 25, 61, 62
Pliny the Younger 24–5, 28–9, 217
Plutarch 75–6
Pollice, Valeria 186
Polybius, Julius 202
Polykleitos 130
Pomona 82
Pompei: Pitture e Mosaici ('Pompeii: Paintings and Mosaics') 44
Pompeii
   archaeological importance of 20–1
   baths in 165–7
   bombing of in World War II 94–5
   ceremonial carriage discovery 123–6
   Christianity in 207–8
   Civita Giuliana discoveries 131–6, 141–2
   and Dionysus 80, 101, 105

INDEX

and Doryphoros of Stabiae 127–31
economic activity in 168–72
erotic imagery in 37–9
eruption sequence 25–9
Etruscan influence on 83–5
everyday life in 143–4, 160–7, 222–3
forgetting of 216–17
Gabriel Zuchtriegel appointed director of 19–20
gaps in archaeology 30–1
Goethe in 29, 72–3
'great dig' at 221–7
Greek influence in 195–7
images of Hermaphroditus in 44, 49–50
and media relationships 138–42
Pliny the Younger on eruption 24–5, 28–9
plundering of 215–16
population estimates 146–52
portrayal of sexual violence 56, 57
private excavations in 97–8
reasons for visiting 5–10
removal of murals from 71–2
residential units in 44, 152–4, 160–3, 164–5
rural population of 155, 160
shops in 163–4
survivors from eruption 215
traditional religions in 83–5
Pompeii Effect 21
Pompey 78
Poppaea Sabina 170, 200, 201, 203, 204–5
population estimates 146–52
Porto Ercolano 95
Porta Marina 95, 165
Portunus 82, 83

Poseidon 34, 54
Postumius 104
Pouzadoux, Claude 91
Python 34

Quirinus 82

Regio IX 222–4
religion
    and Bacchus cult 103–5
    Christianity 75, 102, 115–17, 204–9
    in classical art 68–71, 72–4
    Dionysus 76–80, 101–5, 110, 114–19
    and mystery cults 74–6
    and ritual 90–3, 106
    traditional religions 81–5
residential units 44, 152–4, 160–3, 164–5
Rispoli, Maria 175–6, 187
Ritchie, Hannah 157
Roman Empire
    bathing culture 166
    and classical Greece 31–3, 36–7, 195–7
    and Dionysus 76–80, 101–5
    eroticism in 41–4
    idea of 168
    traditional religions in 81–5
    urban population 155, 156–7
Roscigno Vecchio 145–6
Roser, Max 157

'San Paolino' office complex 148
Sanctuary of Apollo vii, 34
Sarno Baths 165
Sarno Canal 216
Sarno Gate viii, 197
Satyricon, The (Petronius) 54–5, 167, 214
Sauron, Gilles 118, 119

Schola Armaturarum 95
Schwab, Gustav 23
'Secret Cabinet' (National Archaeological Museum) 38
Semele 101, 118
sexual violence 56–8
shops 163–4
Siculus, Diodorus 62
Simone, Nina 184
Sinatra, Frank 184
slaves/slavery 38, 41, 42–3, 53, 79, 135–6, 141–3, 149, 170–1, 189–90, 191–5
Smith, Patti 184
Social War 129
Sophocles 35
Sparagna, Ambrogio 186
Stabiae 129–30, 148
Stabian Baths vii, 165
Stabian Gate viii, 148, 150, 160
Stendhal 3, 5, 8, 9, 10, 16
Stendhal Syndrome 3–4, 5
Stifter, Adalbert 47
Strabo 129

Tacitus 24–5, 203
Temple of Athena viii, 57
Temple of Neptune (Paestum) 14–6, 141–2
Temple of Venus vii, 205
Theatre viii, 184
thermopolia 165
Thermopolium vii
Tiriolo 105
Titus, Emperor 215
Tomb of the Diver (Paestum) 91, 99
Trojan War 223–4

Ukraine 172
urbanisation 155–7

Vastarella, Gianni 186
Velia 177–9
Veneruis Secundio, Marcus 188–94, 197, 198–200, 205
Vettius Conviva, Aulus 51, 53
Vettius Restitutus, Aulus 51, 53
Veyne, Paul 114–17, 119
Via del Vesuvio 80
Via dell'Abbondanza 164
Via di Nola 163
Villa of the Mysteries vii, 74, 79, 91, 92, 93, 95–101, 107–10, 114–16, 117–19, 125
Volturnus 82
Vulcan 82
vulcanology 25

Winckelmann, Johann Joachim 24
World War II 94–6

Zeus 34, 39, 91
Zuchtriegel, Gabriel
    appointed as director of Pompeii 19–20, 176–9
    as archaeology student 14–15, 32
    and Civita Giuliana discoveries 131–6, 141–2
    early interest in classical archaeology 23–4
    at *Gymnasium* 22–3
    and Hermaphroditus 45–8, 49–50
    media relationships 137–42
    opposition to 176–9
    priorities at Pompeii 182–3
    starts work in Italy 86–90
    theatre project 182–8, 217–18